Your Promise Gives Me Life

A Family Devotional Guide about Knowing
and Trusting God's Promises

Your Promise Gives Me Life: A Family Devotional Guide about Knowing and Trusting God's Promises

by Sally Michael

Our vision at Truth78 is that the next generations know, honor, and treasure God, setting their hope in Christ alone, so that they will live as faithful disciples for the glory of God. Our mission is to inspire and equip the church and the home for the comprehensive discipleship of the next generation.

We equip churches and parents by producing curricula for Sunday School, Midweek Bible, Intergenerational, Youth, and Backyard Bible Club settings; vision-casting and training resources (many available free on our website) for both the church and the home; materials and training to help parents in their role in discipling children; and the Fighter Verses™ Bible memory program to encourage the lifelong practice and love of Bible memory.

Published in the United States of America by Truth78.

ISBN: 978-1-952783-58-6

Truth:78

Equipping the Next Generations to Know, Honor, and Treasure God

Truth78.org
info@Truth78.org
(877) 400-1414

Table of Contents

Preface

Do you love to see the tulips and daffodils poking up through the soil? They are announcing that spring is coming. New life is blooming! Things are being renewed! The cold winter nights are over, the snow has been stored away for another season, and green leaves will soon open on the trees!

God's promises are like the tulips and daffodils of spring. They bring new life into tired souls. They renew our hope and strengthen weary saints. They help us to stand strong and true against the sweeping tides of changing ideas. They bring words and vision to our prayers. They encourage us that "Weeping may tarry for the night, but joy comes with the morning!"[1] God's glorious enduring promises give us life!

One of the greatest means of fighting the fight of faith is to cling to the precious promises of God. There is a promise for every trial we endure, every emotion we feel, and every temptation we face. God's promises are a sword and a shield for the soul. But, like any other spiritual weapon, God's promises languish in our souls if we do not *know* them and *trust* them. We cannot find refuge in God's promises if we are unfamiliar with them.

This book has been written to encourage your family to study God's promises, memorize them, store them in your soul, run to them in time of need, pray them, and trust them when the winds of adversity blow. They will breathe new life into your soul.

> *Have you not known? Have you not heard? The LORD is the everlasting God, the Creator of the ends of the earth. He does not faint or grow weary; his understanding is unsearchable. [29]He gives power to the faint, and to him who has no might he increases strength. [30]Even youths shall faint and be weary, and young men shall fall exhausted; [31]but they who wait for the LORD shall renew their strength; they shall mount up with wings like eagles; they shall run and not be weary; they shall walk and not faint. (Isaiah 40:28-31)*

> *This is my comfort in my affliction, that your promise gives me life. (Psalm 119:50)*

---

1 Psalm 30:5b

How to Use this Devotional

It is our hope that this resource will help your family spend some time around the Word and create opportunities for spiritual discussion throughout the days and weeks that follow. You can put as much or as little time and effort into this devotional time as your life permits. Some of the ongoing discussion may happen more intentionally around the kitchen table or informally as you go through your days together.

The elements of this devotional are:

Ask: This is simply a quick starter question (or questions) to launch the topic of the verse. Then read the introduction to the verse and the verse itself. If you have younger children, you may need to define some of the words in the Bible verse.

Discuss: Ask as many questions as time and your children's attention spans permit. Discuss them to any depth you desire. You can pick and choose questions or ask them all. Some of the questions are more suited for older children and some for younger ones. But even younger children can benefit from all the questions and answers if you rephrase them more simply or explain them.

Read: Read the short devotional. There are two versions to choose from—the first one for parents and older children, the second one for younger children. If your children have a wide span of ages, you may want to read the summary for the older children first and then have an older child read to the younger children the summary intended for them. Or you may choose to read the younger children's summary first and then follow up with the older children's summary.

Pray: End with prayer. There is a suggested prayer topic for you as the parent, but you may want to encourage your children to pray about the topic of the devotional as well. You may want to encourage your children to pray using the verse highlighted in the devotional.

Optional: Encourage your whole family to memorize the verse. A memorized verse will not only give your children truths to ponder when the verse comes to mind, but it is also a means to fight the fight of faith.

Note: God is faithful to keep His promises to His children. But your children may not yet be saved. Keep confronting your children with the blessing of being God's child and the claim that His children have on His promises, without assuming that your children are at this point true believers. Unless you are convinced that your children are saved, continue to pray for their salvation while you acquaint your children with the promises of God. Keep holding out the hope of the gospel to your children as you discuss spiritual truths from the devotional guide.

It is our prayer that you may experience a time of spiritual bonding as a family around God's Word, and that His promises might be a means of strengthening your faith.

God's Goodness

Ask

What good thing happened to you today?

This good thing and every good thing that happens to you is a gift from God who is good to all people.

> *The LORD is good to all, and his mercy is over all that he has made. (Psalm 145:9)*

Discuss

- LORD (in all capital letters) is the way our English Bibles record God's personal name, *Yahweh.* Yahweh means self-sufficient, almighty, unchanging, sovereign, and eternal. How does this name give credibility to the phrase, "The LORD is good to all"? (How do each of these characteristics enable God to be good to all?)

- How is God good to all? (In what ways is God good to everyone?)

- "Mercy" is kindness or favor given to those who are undeserving because we are sinners. What does the second half of the verse tell you about what God is like?

- What are some of the blessings God has brought into your life? (How has God been good to you?) Sometimes the things that don't seem good are, in fact, good for us. Is there something in your life that, at first, you didn't think was good, but in the end you saw that it actually was good?

Read

It is astounding that God is good to *everyone.* Every single person is undeserving of the mercy of God, and yet, God extends His mercy to all. What a merciful and gracious God we have!

His goodness is shown in the hundreds of promises He makes to His people in the Bible—each one of them a promise to do good to us and to be the kind of God who is worthy of our admiration and praise. Each promise is like a present from God—some for everyone and others for His people alone. Each promise is certain, given by the One who has placed His rainbow in the sky as a sign of His promise-keeping.

For Younger Children: It is amazing that God is good to *everyone.* No one deserves the kindness of God, and yet God is kind to everyone. What a good and kind God we have!

We see His goodness in the hundreds of promises He makes to His people in the Bible. Every promise is a promise to do good to us. Every promise shows us that God deserves to be loved and praised by us. God will keep every single one of His promises. His rainbow in the sky is a sign that He is a promise-keeping God.

Pray

Praise God for His glorious promises and His sure character that seals them. Pray that you will have faith to believe that God is good and merciful, and pray that you may trust Him for the fulfillment of His promises to you.

Promises to Believers

Ask

What privileges or benefits do you have as a member of your family? How is this different from what your friend receives from your family? What did you do to receive these special privileges and benefits?

It is possible to be not only a member of your family but to be a member of God's family as well!

> *But to all who did receive him, who believed in his name, he gave the right to become children of God, (John 1:12)*

Discuss

- What is the difference between knowing someone and trusting someone? What does trust in Jesus look like? (Receiving and believing in Jesus can be understood as trusting in Jesus.)

- The name "Jesus" comes from the Hebrew name, *Yeshua,* which means "to deliver" or "to rescue." What does this suggest that we must believe about Jesus? What does He rescue us from?

- To "become" means that something new has happened to change what was before. What is the promise in this verse? What has changed, and how did it change?[2]

- Have you received Jesus as your Savior? If so, tell your family about this. (What did God use to draw you to Himself?)

---

2 A person's standing before God has changed. Before he was alienated from God; now he is accepted into God's family. His sins are forgiven and he is declared *righteous*–right before God. His sin is not counted or held against him because he is trusting in Jesus' completed sin-bearing work on the cross.

Read

God made a wonderful promise to Abram—to be his God! *God* promised to enter into an everlasting covenant relationship with Abram, and to bless him...and his offspring throughout all generations.[3] What an incredible promise of blessing to the covenant people! God will not turn away from them; He will strengthen and help them, take them by the hand, keep them, and never forget them.

We would despair if the only way to inherit this covenant relationship and the accompanying promises is through bloodlines. We would be without hope. But thanks be to God! He invites us to participate in this covenant relationship and inherit the promises through adoption into His family through faith in Jesus! All who receive Jesus, who believe in His name have the right to become the children of God! We are the inheritors of God's promises to His children! We who are sons of Abraham by faith have an everlasting covenant with God.

For Younger Children: God made a wonderful promise to Abraham (then called Abram). He promised to be Abraham's God! God promised to have a special relationship with Abraham forever. He promised to do good to Abraham, his children, his grandchildren, and all their children—everyone in Abraham's family would be part of God's family. What a wonderful promise this is to God's people! God will never leave them or turn away from them. He will help them, protect them, and never forget them.

It would be very sad if the only way to be part of God's family was to be born into Abraham's family. We would have no hope of receiving God's promises or being part of God's family. How wonderful it is that God has promised that we can be part of His family and receive all His promises by adoption! We don't have to be born into Abraham's family. We can be part of God's family through faith in Jesus! By trusting in Jesus to be our Savior we can become children of God! Then all of God's promises can be ours. God's children will be part of His family forever.

---

3 Genesis 17:1-8

Pray

This week, if you are trusting Jesus as your Savior, thank God for your inheritance as a child of God, a member of God's family, a recipient of blessing, an heir to the promises. Pray that your children would receive and believe in Jesus and become adopted into the family of God.

Promises to Unbelievers

Ask

There are many different ways we could separate people into groups—those who like chocolate and those who don't, those who are musical and those who are not, those who live north of the equator and those who live south of it. What other ways could we separate people into groups?

God only has one way of separating people, and He separates them into one of two groups.

> *for the LORD knows the way of the righteous, but the way of the wicked will perish. (Psalm 1:6)*

Discuss

- From God's perspective, there are only two groups of people. What are they?[4]

- Who are the "righteous"? Who are the "wicked"? What promises does God make to each of these groups of people?

- What happens when a person or a criminal disobeys the law and is found guilty? Why is it right for there to be consequences or punishment for breaking the law?

- Has God warned people of the consequences of breaking His holy law? Explain. Did God *have* to give people a way of escaping His just punishment? What does this tell you about God?[5]

---

4 You may want to read Matthew 5:31-34, 41.
5 See Romans 5:8.

- What is the difference between knowing about God and honoring God? Do you think that you know about God, or that you honor God?

- Are there unbelievers your family can pray for? What plan can you make to regularly pray for these people?

Read

God is good to all, causing the sun to shine and rain to fall on the just and the unjust (Matthew 5:45). This is a remarkable statement of the character of God, who is good even to His enemies. Yet God's kindness to unrepentant sinners does not last forever. There will come a time of reckoning, and the unjust will suffer eternal pain and torment.

Jesus Himself will do a great sorting at the end of the age, separating His sheep from the unbelieving goats (Matthew 25:32). His judgment will be final and His punishment eternal. Hell is a place of great pain and suffering, but it is a just punishment for those who rebel against God and refuse to repent. Judgment is final. There is no passage between hell and heaven.[6] This should motivate us to pray for unbelievers. Have you thought seriously about your own standing before God?

For Younger Children: God is good to everyone. He gives sunshine and rain to all people—good people and even bad people. What a great God He is! He is even good to His enemies. But God's kindness to sinful people who do not turn away from sin does not last forever. The day will come when those who do not trust Jesus and love God will be punished forever.

At the end of time, Jesus will separate His children from those who do not love Him. Everyone who has not trusted in Jesus as their Savior will be punished in hell. Hell is a place of great pain and suffering. There is no way to get out of hell. So we should pray for those who do not love Jesus.

---

6   Jesus often told stories to illustrate spiritual truth. The story of the rich man and Lazarus in Luke 16:19-26, though not a real event, nevertheless portrays some sobering truths.

What group do you want to be in—the group that trusts Jesus and goes to heaven or the group that is punished forever?

Pray

Praise God for His rescue in Jesus of undeserving sinners. Thank Him that He watches over the way of the righteous. Pray for your children to consider their spiritual standing and the warning to unbelievers. Ask God to save your children.

God Always Keeps His Promises

Ask

Have you ever broken a promise, or has someone broken a promise made to you? Why was this promise broken? Was it on purpose, or was there something you or the other person could not control?

Unlike the limitations on people, God is not limited by anything—nothing is outside His control. So when God makes a promise, He always keeps it. Nothing can stop Him from keeping His Word.

> *"God is not man, that he should lie, or a son of man, that he should change his mind. Has he said, and will he not do it? Or has he spoken, and will he not fulfill it?" (Numbers 23:19)*

Discuss

- What are some of the differences between God and man? What do you know about God that shows you that He can be trusted to keep His promises?

- What repetitions[7] do you see in Numbers 23:19? Why does this verse have so many repetitions? (What is the point?)

- Can you think of any reason why God could not or would not keep His promises?

- Is there something we can pray about as a family? Can you think of a promise of God that would help our family?

---

7   You may need to explain that a "repetition" is saying the same thing more than once, even though it may be in different words.

Read

Although we try to keep our promises, sometimes we just can't. Unforeseen things come up, our abilities are less than we anticipated, and we are limited in many ways. But God has no limitations, no hidden agendas, and no needs. He is completely free to keep His promises. All His wonderful attributes commend Him as a promise-keeping God. His promises are reliable because His character is reliable. What wonderful assurance there is for us that we can confidently count on His promises!

This week, assess your confidence in God's promises. Is your confidence reflective of the quality of His character? Do you really believe God is who He says He is? Ask God to increase your faith this week so you can confidently face your days with the assurance and conviction that God will do what He says He will do.

For Younger Children: We try to keep our promises, but sometimes we just can't. Things happen that we didn't know would happen. We are not able to do what we thought we could do. We are not strong enough or smart enough. Maybe we forget or change our minds. But that never happens with God. God can do anything; nothing can stop God. So God can keep all His promises. Everything about God—His power, His wisdom, His truthfulness, His goodness, everything He is—shows us that He will keep His promises. We can be sure of this because we know what God is like!

This week think about how much you trust in God to keep His promises. Do you really believe that He is who He says He is and that He will do what He says He will do? Ask God this week to give you a stronger faith in Him. Ask Him to help you to trust that He will do what He says He will do.

Pray

Thank God for His inscrutable character, which backs up every one of His promises. Pray that your children will see that God is trustworthy, and His promises are sure.

DAY 5

Conditional Promises

Ask

Some promises have conditions or requirements placed on them. They are like agreements. For example: "If you finish your homework, you can go to your friend's house." A promise is made—that you can go to your friend's house. But there is a condition or requirement—you first have to finish your homework. Give some examples of conditional promises or agreements.

Some of God's promises have conditions. God will always keep His promise if the condition is met. But if the condition is not met, God is not obligated to keep His promise. Below is an example of one of God's conditional promises.

> *"But this command I gave them: 'Obey my voice, and I will be your God, and you shall be my people. And walk in all the way that I command you, that it may be well with you.'" (Jeremiah 7:23)*

Discuss

- What is the promise and the condition in the conditional promises below?

  - 1 John 1:9—If we confess our sins, he is faithful and just to forgive us our sins and to cleanse us from all unrighteousness.

  - Matthew 6:14—"For if you forgive others their trespasses, your heavenly Father will also forgive you,"

  - Isaiah 26:3—You keep him in perfect peace whose mind is stayed on you, because he trusts in you.

  - Matthew 10:32—"So everyone who acknowledges me before men, I also will acknowledge before my Father who is in heaven,"

- What promise did God make with Israel according to Jeremiah 7:23? What is the condition? Did Israel keep the condition? What was the result?

- Does God have the right to make conditions for His promises? Why?

- Would God ever decide that He didn't want to keep His promise anymore? How do you know this?

- Do we have a right to expect God to keep a conditional promise when we don't keep our part of it? Explain. What do we miss out on or lose when we disobey God?

Read

God is faithful to all His promises...but we are not always faithful. Some of God's promises of blessing are accompanied by conditions that must be met in order for the promise to be fulfilled. God's promises are completely trustworthy, but sometimes we fail to keep the condition and the promise is not fulfilled because of our disobedience.

This is what happened to Israel. While Joshua led Israel, the people walked in God's ways and received great blessings, defeating their enemies in battle and possessing their land. But after Joshua died, each man "did what was right in his own eyes" (e.g., Judges 17:6). Israel walked in disobedience, worshiping other gods and breaking God's commands. When this happened, God's promise of success ended because His conditions were not met.

Yet, God was still faithful to Israel, repeating His promise to bless Israel even as long as almost 800 years later.

> "But this command I gave them: 'Obey my voice, and I will be your God, and you shall be my people. And walk in all the way that I command you, that it may be well with you.'" (Jeremiah 7:23)

What a gracious and good God we have—a God who is eager to bless His people if they would just walk in His ways.

For Younger Children: God always keeps His promises, but we don't always keep ours. Some of God's promises have conditions or requirements that we must keep. We can trust God to always keep His part of a conditional promise. But sometimes we do not receive the blessings of God's promise because we don't keep the condition—we don't do our part.

This is what happened to Israel. When Joshua led Israel, the people obeyed God's conditions, and God helped them win battles and have their own country. But after Joshua died, the people worshiped other gods and disobeyed God's commandments. So they lost the blessing that God would have given them. Their enemies defeated them in battles, and they were taken away to other countries.

But God was still faithful to His people and even gave them His promise again 800 years later.

Pray

Thank God for His promise of blessing to His people and His faithfulness to His promises. Ask Him to give you an obedient heart. Pray that your children will see the benefit of obeying God and have a desire to walk in His ways.

Promise: Salvation for All Who Call

Ask

If someone you knew called out to you, would you answer? If someone needed help, called out, and you were able to help, would you? Why?

God is more gracious, kind, polite, thoughtful, and more able to help people than we are. If we, who are sinners, would answer someone who calls, how much more would God answer?

> *"...everyone who calls upon the name of the Lord shall be saved."* (Acts 2:21b)

Discuss

- What is the promise in this verse? What is the condition?

- What does it mean to call on the name of the Lord?[8]

- What does it mean to save someone?

- Why does man need to be saved?[9]

- How does God save sinners?[10]

- What does salvation save us **from**?[11]

- What does salvation save us **for**?[12]

- Is God's salvation for you? Explain.[13]

---

8 To call out to God for help: "Jesus, I need You. I am a sinner and cannot take my sins away myself. Please forgive my sins."

9 God is holy. He is without sin. All people have sinned and deserve God's anger at sin and punishment. Sinners cannot come near to a holy God.

10 Jesus took the punishment sinful man deserved and made a way for sinners to be forgiven.

11 It saves us from God's anger at sin and punishment for sin.

12 Salvation is being saved, guarded, and kept for life in heaven with God forever.

13 Your child should be able to give a credible profession of faith, or acknowledge that he is not yet saved or is unsure of his salvation. You may want to talk about evidences of saving faith in the life of a believer to help your child discern his spiritual standing. Encourage your child to ask God to show him if he is saved.

Read

How often we fail to be astounded by the gift of salvation? If we have lived with this truth for any length of time, it is easy to take it for granted. Yet, it should fill us with awe, gratitude, and praise that God accepts everyone who calls on His name! This profound truth should humble us. Who are we to receive this most precious gift?

Every sin is washed away at the cross! Every wrong heart attitude, unholy thought, sinful action is gone, covered by the blood of Jesus for *anyone* who calls on the name of the Lord. God's grace to sinners saves us *from* His anger at sin and punishment for sin, and saves us *for* eternal life with Him in heaven!

All of this is found in Jesus—in Jesus alone—who will never cast out any sincere seeker. Are you rejoicing in this amazing grace today? Are you astounded by God's gift of salvation?

For Younger Children: It is easy to forget how *amazing* it is that Jesus died on the cross for our sins. We hear the story so often. But it should still amaze us that God accepts everyone who calls on His name. Why should we receive such a precious gift? We don't deserve it. Praise God for His kindness to sinners!

If you are trusting in Jesus as your Savior, every sin is forgiven. Every wrong attitude, bad thought, and mean or wrong thing we have done is taken away by Jesus for *anyone* who calls on Him! God's kindness to sinners saves us *from* His anger at sin and punishment for sin. It saves us *for* life forever with Him in heaven!

You can find salvation and love in Jesus, who will never turn away anyone who seeks Him. This is an amazing gift from God!

Pray

Pray that God will grab your heart anew with the great news of the gospel. Ask Him to replace apathy with enthusiasm, indifference with gratitude, and familiarity with new eyes to see His marvelous grace. Pray that your children will catch a glimpse of the amazing grace of God that would offer the gift of salvation to anyone who calls on His name.

Promise: God Will Forgive You

Ask

What is the dirtiest, grubbiest, smelliest you have ever been? How did you get that way? What were you doing? How did it feel then to have a fresh, clean, hot shower or bath?

In a way, that is what Jesus does for our souls. He takes our dirty, grubby, smelly souls full of sin and wipes them clean!

> *If we confess our sins, he is faithful and just to forgive us our sins and to cleanse us from all unrighteousness. (1 John 1:9)*

Discuss

- What are the two different ways God will deal with our sin?[14]

- What is the wonderful promise in this verse? How can you be sure that God will keep this promise?[15]

- What is the condition to this promise? What does it mean to confess our sins?[16]

- What do we often do about our sin rather than admit it?[17]

- Why is it so hard for us to admit our sins? (What prevents us from admitting and confessing our sins?)

- What is the result of admitting our sin to God? What does God's forgiveness look like?[18]

---

14 God will condemn us for it or forgive us.
15 God's faithfulness and His justice ensure that He will keep this promise. God always does what He says He will do—He is faithful. God is just—what He has determined is the condition for receiving His forgiveness and cleansing. God will not change; He will honor His Word.
16 Be sure your child knows the difference between repentance and true confession versus just feeling bad about the consequences of sin.
17 We make excuses, deny it, ignore it.
18 He will not hold our sins against us. He removes them far from us. He blots them out. See Psalm 103:8-14; Isaiah 43:25; and Micah 7:19.

- What is the wonderful promise in this verse? How can you be sure that God will keep this promise?

- What is the condition to this promise?

- Is there anything you need to ask forgiveness for?

Read

Amazing: It's a word we use too glibly to describe things that really aren't amazing. But grace: that *is* amazing...and sweet. *Amazing grace, how sweet the sound...*It is when we realize that we are wretches that we realize how very amazing God's grace is—His grace that forgives the unforgiveable, despicable, rebellious, apathetic attitudes of our hearts, and the actions we perform and words we fling out. We can't change our attitudes, pay for our actions, or take back our words. But worse than that, we can't erase the offense of our sin against our Holy God.

This is where grace comes in...

> *1 John 1:9—If we confess our sins, he is faithful and just to forgive us our sins and to cleanse us from all unrighteousness.*

> *Isaiah 43:25—"I, I am he who blots out your transgressions for my own sake, and I will not remember your sins."*

Forgiveness full and free coming from God our Father, cleansing complete and refreshing from Jesus our Savior...eagerly: This is *amazing*. Like the woman caught in adultery, Jesus says to every sincere confessor, "Neither do I condemn you" (John 8:11). God's promise to forgive repentant sinners is precious. And grace is... *amazing*.

For Younger Children: We use the word amazing too much. We use it for things that really aren't amazing; they are just different than what is ordinary or normal. What is really amazing—greater than we can ever understand—is God's grace. When we truly understand how awful our sins are, we begin to understand the greatness of God's kindness to undeserving sinners. He forgives the ugliest, most rebellious, most awful attitudes in our hearts, and things we do and words we say. We can't change our heart attitudes, make up for the wrong things we do, or take back our unkind words. But what is worse is that we can't erase our sins and how we have offended and grieved God.

But God is kind to sinners who come to Him. His grace is amazing. We don't deserve it, but God will completely forgive us when we honestly admit our sin to Him and ask for His forgiveness. God's promise to forgive us when we truly want to turn away from sin is a precious promise. And His grace is...*amazing.*

Pray

This week, thank God for His forgiveness full and free. Ask Him to reveal any unconfessed sin and to give you a repentant heart. Pray that the children in your family get a sense that they too are "wretches" and in need of God's forgiveness. Ask God to give them humble and repentant hearts.

Promise: God Will Be with You

Ask

Can you remember a time when you were little and were worried or scared about something—like sliding down a big slide, crossing a busy street, or going down to a dark basement? When you have to do something hard or a little scary, how is it helpful if someone is with you?

God knew that Joshua would be nervous or scared about leading the people of Israel across the Jordan River to conquer the land of Canaan. So He gave Joshua a promise. This same promise is for all those who are trusting in Him.

> *"Have I not commanded you? Be strong and courageous. Do not be frightened, and do not be dismayed, for the LORD your God is with you wherever you go." (Joshua 1:9)*

Discuss

- How does this verse show you that God is understanding? Was He mad at Joshua for being afraid? How do you know that?

- What reason did God give Joshua for not being afraid? What did God promise Joshua? What does He promise His children (Christians)?

- Can you think of some times in the Bible when God was with His people? What did He do? What does it mean that God is with His children wherever they go?[19]

---

19 Make sure your children understand that God is not just idly standing by, but He is actively helping, protecting, guiding, and caring for His children.

- What kinds of things do you have to do that make you a little afraid or worried?

- How can knowing that God is with you everywhere you go help you? (How can it give you strength and courage?)

Read

God fills heaven and earth. So, just as it is foolish to think that you can get away from the air in a room, it is also foolish to think that you can get away from God. For those who do not know God, this can be a scary thought. God sees every thought, every intention of the heart, and every deed. For those whose sins are not covered by the blood of Jesus, to be in the constant presence of God is not comforting.

But to those who know God, who have a deep and abiding friendship with Him, it is a source of continual comfort that no matter where we are at any time of day, we have the assurance that God is with us. He will not leave us or forsake us. No matter where we go, He is there with us.

He is with us, not just standing idly by, but actively engaged in helping His children. We can count on His continual, attentive presence with us.

What are you facing today? What fears or worries do you have? As you go through this week, remind yourself that the God of the universe, your heavenly Father, is *with you.* You are not alone. His mighty hand is with you, His loving heart guides you, and His watchful eye is ever watching over you.

For Younger Children: God is everywhere—He fills heaven and earth. So He sees us wherever we are. God knows everything we think, feel, and do. He sees all our sins. If you do not have a friendship with God, this can be a scary thought.

But if you have a friendship with God, you know that God is on your side. Your God is with you no matter where you are all day long to help you, guide you, forgive you, comfort you, protect you, and watch over you. What a wonderful thing that is! God never leaves us! He is not just watching from far away, but He is right here with us, helping us and loving us!

Are you afraid or worried about anything? Remind yourself that the all-powerful God of the universe is right there. And if you are His child, He is your heavenly Father who loves you and is always watching over you.

Pray

Thank God for His continual presence with you. Ask Him to remind you to walk in constant fellowship with Him throughout your week. Pray that your children will have a strong awareness of whether the thought of God's presence with them brings them comfort or concern. Pray that they will depend on Him this week.

Promise: Nothing Can Separate You from God's Love

Ask

If you are careful, you can separate the egg yolk from the egg white in a raw egg. It is even easier to do this with a hard-boiled egg! What else can be separated or taken apart from each other?[20]

The Bible tells us about something that can never be separated.

> *For I am sure that neither death nor life, nor angels nor rulers, nor things present nor things to come, nor powers, [39]nor height nor depth, nor anything else in all creation, will be able to separate us from the love of God in Christ Jesus our Lord. (Romans 8:38-39)*

Discuss

- What is the promise in this verse? Who is the "us"? (Who is this promise for?)

- When Paul wrote this verse, rulers and leaders were treating Christians very badly. They were causing all kinds of problems for Christians and hurting Christians. Some Christians were even being killed. Why would this verse give hope and comfort to these Christians?

- When hard things happen in our lives, does this mean that God doesn't love us anymore? Explain.[21]

---

20 For example: an orange and the peel; cream filling from a sandwich cookie; frosting from a cake; two fighting kids

21 Make sure that your children understand that suffering is not a sign that God does not love Christians. God does not protect Christians from all hardships, but He is there with them in the hardships.

- After Jesus was arrested, how did Peter answer when he was asked if he knew Jesus?[22] What does it do to a friendship when you betray a friend? After His resurrection, how did Jesus treat Peter?[23] What does this tell you about Jesus?

- Does your sin separate you from God?[24]

- How can this verse be an encouragement to you?

Read

In the face of first-century persecution, Paul's words that nothing can separate a follower of Christ from the love of God were very comforting. Not tribulation, distress, persecution, famine, nakedness, danger, sword, death, life, angels, rulers, past things, present things, powers, height, depth…nothing in all creation can diminish the love that God has for His children. These were Paul's words from a Roman prison…and Peter's experience after denying Jesus three times.

On the beach after the resurrection, Peter was not banished from the friendship of the risen Christ. He was welcomed, forgiven, restored, and even entrusted with the ministry of reconciling sinners to Christ. What a gracious, merciful God we have!

Peter's denial was not a temporary lapse of memory or an impulsive response but a steadfast, repeated denial that he was a follower of Christ. Yet, at the gaze of Jesus, Peter saw the sinfulness of his heart, the grief his sin caused, and the anguish of his Lord…and Peter wept bitterly over his sin.

As with Peter, our sin grieves our Savior…but God never leaves us or forsakes us, and He surrounds us with steadfast love. Do we rejoice in the steadfast love of the Lord, which never ceases? What is our attitude toward our sin? Does it grieve us that it grieves our Lord? Do we weep bitterly over our sin, and then stand in amazement that we are not separated from the love of God?

---

22 Matthew 26:69-75
23 John 21:15-17
24 This is a bit of a trick question. Unrepentant sinners who are not trusting in Jesus as their Savior are definitely separated from God due to their sin. They are condemned. They are not separated from His goodness in that God is good to all. Christians who have unconfessed sin have placed a barrier between themselves and God. They are not separated from the love of God in that God is steadfast in His love for His children. But God is grieved by their sin and will discipline them to bring about repentance and fellowship with Him.

For Younger Children: If you are not trusting in Jesus as your Savior, your sin separates or keeps you apart from God. Only trusting in Jesus alone for forgiveness will fix the broken friendship between God and a sinner.

But if you are a child of God, nothing will ever separate you from God's love. Difficult things may happen to Christians, but they will never lose God's love. Even though Peter denied Jesus, Jesus forgave him. Peter saw the sinfulness of his heart and the sadness his sin caused, and he cried over his sin. Jesus welcomed Peter as a friend again and even trusted him to be His disciple to preach the gospel.

Our sin causes sadness to Jesus too...but He never turns away from His children. Instead, He surrounds His children with never-ending love. It is amazing that, even when Christians sin, we are not separated from the love of God. But our sin does make Him sad. Does it make you sad, too?

Pray

This week, thank God that nothing in all creation can separate you from the love of God if you are His child. Examine your heart and turn from anything that would grieve your Savior. Pray that your children would desire to be included in those who can never be separated from the love of God in Christ.

Promise: God Will Complete His Work in You

Ask

What kind of projects do you like to work on? What are some projects you have finished? Do you always finish your projects?

Unlike us, God always completes His work.

> *...he who began a good work in you will bring it to completion at the day of Jesus Christ. (Philippians 1:6b)*

Discuss

- What is the "good work" this verse is referring to?[25]

- What important truth do you see in the first phrase (eight words)? Why can these words give us confidence?[26]

- Since becoming like Christ is God at work in us, does this mean we can sit back and just let Him work? Why not? Explain.

- How will Christians be different after God completes His work when Jesus returns?

- How does Satan fight against you?

- What are you most looking forward to being freed from? (What sins, temptations, or weaknesses will be gone at the return of Jesus if you are a child of God?)

---

25 1 John 3:2
26 Make sure your children understand that the work of faith in a Christian's life is initiated by God. Since God is the one at work, we can be confident that He will accomplish that which He promises.

Read

Do you ever feel discouraged at how far you are from having the character of Christ? God's Word gives us tremendous words of hope in the promise of Philippians 1:6b. God began a good work in every Christian...and He will finish it! He, Himself, is conforming His children to the image of His Son. This is not dependent on our self-effort, but it is the work of the indwelling Holy Spirit. This is good news!

In the last lesson, we saw Peter's failure to stand with Jesus when he denied Him three times...and Jesus' forgiveness and faithfulness to Peter. In this lesson, we see a different Peter—the Peter after the Holy Spirit descended upon him and filled him at Pentecost. This was part of God's completing work in Peter. The Holy Spirit transformed him from a weak, fearful, disloyal disciple to a strong, bold, loyal defender of the faith! This time Peter is not cowering in fear, afraid to acknowledge his friendship with Jesus. He is boldly preaching after being thrown into prison and being threatened with suffering if he continues.

What is the secret to Peter's transformation? Satan wanted to sift Peter,[27] but Jesus had prayed for him. And God answered, sending the Holy Spirit to empower Peter and the other disciples...and all believers.[28] This is the same Holy Spirit who dwells in the soul of every Christian. God's promise stands true for you. He will complete His work in you. He will transform you into the image of His Son!

For Younger Children: We can be very discouraged by the sin in our lives. We are not like Jesus in so many ways. But this verse gives great hope to Christians. If you are a child of God, He is working to free you from the sins that you struggle with. This comes through the work of the Holy Spirit in you. When Jesus returns, the struggle will be over, and God will complete His work of making you completely free from sin!

Do you remember the story about Peter denying Jesus three times? Jesus forgave Peter, and at Pentecost the Holy Spirit

---

27 Luke 22:31-32
28 Acts 2

came upon Peter. Peter was changed from a weak, fearful, disloyal disciple into a strong, bold, loyal defender of the faith! He boldly preached even after he was thrown in jail and told he could not preach when they let him go.[29]

Satan wanted to destroy Peter, but Jesus had prayed for Peter and God sent the Holy Spirit to make Peter strong in faith. The same Holy Spirit who is every Christian's helper strengthens us. If you are a child of God, God promises to change you to have the character of Jesus.

Pray

This week, thank God that He is faithful and will finish the work He has begun in your life as a Christian. Ask Him to begin that work in unsaved children in your home or life. Pray that saved children in your home or life would desire the kind of God-transforming work in their lives that they see in Peter's life.

---

29 Acts 4:1-20

Promise: You Will Bear Fruit

Ask

What are your favorite fruits? Do you have any special memories associated (connected) with any of them?[30]

The Bible talks about fruit, too. But it is a different kind of fruit.

> *"I am the vine; you are the branches. Whoever abides in me and I in him, he it is that bears much fruit, for apart from me you can do nothing." (John 15:5)*

Discuss

- What is so important about the vine in comparison to the branches? Why does Jesus call Himself the Vine?

- Who are the branches in this verse?[31]

- What does it mean to abide in Jesus?[32] Why can true good fruit only come through a trusting relationship with Jesus.[33]

- Jesus is referring to two kinds of fruit. What are they?[34]

- What good fruit do you see in yourself or in others?

---

30 For example: Eating watermelon on a hot summer day; picking strawberries; eating mangos at my cousin's house
31 Make sure your children understand that the branches are Christians, and that God's promises to Christians are not for everyone, but are for followers of Jesus.
32 It means to depend on Him, to trust Him, to look to Him for help
33 True fruit comes from right hearts. Only the Holy Spirit can give Christians the right heart to have true good fruit for God's glory.
34 The fruit of the Spirit (Galatians 5:22-23) and good works (John 15:5; Ephesians 2:10)

Read

How often we try to live the Christian life on our own. Yet Jesus reminds us that He is the Vine, and we are just the branches. In the face of our sense of self-sufficient pride, He reminds us that "apart from me you can do nothing." This is a much-needed reminder of our dependency on Jesus. Yes, it humbles us...but it should also give us hope. Our fruit is produced by Jesus Himself. He sustains, empowers, encourages, and equips us! This is good news! Abiding in the Vine causes fruit to grow!

The fruit produced by abiding in Jesus is both the fruit of the Spirit—love, joy, peace, patience, kindness, goodness, faithfulness, gentleness, self-control (Galatians 5:22-23)—and the fruit of good works. The Holy Spirit produces in the Christian true good works, not the self-serving, selfish good works that call attention to ourselves and serve our own interests, but the true good works that "give glory to [our] Father who is in heaven" (Matthew 5:16). True good works are those done by God's people, with God's heart, for God's glory. This is why they can only be done through the work of the Holy Spirit by abiding in Jesus.

> *"In the same way let your light shine before others, so that they may see your good works and give glory to your Father who is in heaven." (Matthew 5:16)*

For Younger Children: We cannot live the Christian life on our own. We need Jesus. We cannot produce any good fruit unless Jesus is at work in our hearts. He is the Vine that gives His children strength, encouragement, and ability.

The fruit that Jesus works in His children is the fruit of the Spirit—love, joy, peace, patience, kindness, goodness, faithfulness, gentleness, and self-control. Jesus also helps His children to do true good works. This is not when we do something good so that others will like us or so that we will get something from someone. True good works are done to bring glory to God—to show His greatness and worth. True good works can only be done by depending on Jesus.

Pray

This week, ask God to give you a humble heart of dependency on Jesus, and then to provide opportunities for your light to shine before others. Pray that your children will understand what true good works are, so that they are confronted with the reality of their need to be connected to the true Vine.

Promise: God Hears Your Prayers

Ask

If someone you knew called out to you, would you answer that person or ignore him? Why?

It is polite for a person to answer when someone he knows calls him. God is polite and does not ignore His children when they cry out to Him.

> *The eyes of the LORD are toward the righteous and his ears toward their cry. (Psalm 34:15)*

Discuss

- Does God have eyes and ears? What does the Bible mean in this verse when it talks about God's eyes and ears?

- God is attentive—He is always aware of His children's needs and always answers them when they cry out to Him. Does this mean that God always answers in the way we expect Him to? Explain.[35]

- How can you be sure that God always answers His children when they pray?[36]

- Tell us about an answer to prayer you experienced.

---

35 Make sure your children understand that God always answers the prayers of His children, but His answer could be "Yes," "No," or "Wait."

36 Make sure your children understand that God's Word says He will always answer, and everything in the Word is true regardless of how things appear. See 1 Peter 3:12; Proverbs 15:29; John 9:31; and 1 John 5:14-15.

Read

The story of Elijah and the prophets of Baal[37] is a favorite because it shows God's power and reveals His superiority over anyone or anything that would claim His throne. It also shows His attentiveness to the call of His children. As Elijah heckles the prophets about the inattentiveness of Baal, we are reminded that God is always attentive to the call of His children. His promise to answer prayer is a great and glorious promise. He hears us when we pray! Every time!

> *The eyes of the LORD are toward the righteous and his ears toward their cry. (Psalm 34:15)*

It is the great privilege of Christians to bring every need to God with the reassurance that He hears and answers that prayer. But prayer is more than just asking for God's blessing; it is also praising Him, thanking Him, and confessing our sins. How important it is to remember all these aspects of prayer as we fellowship with our God.

Though God does not always answer the way we want Him to, He does always answer our prayers. His answer is always right—whether it be "Yes," "No," or "Wait"—as God always acts for the good of His children.

For Younger Children: Do you remember the story of Elijah and the prophets of Baal? What happened when the prophets of Baal called out to their god? Nothing! But what happened when Elijah called out to the one true God? God answered with fire from heaven and burned the offering! God always hears and answers the call of His children. What a great promise this is!

> *The eyes of the LORD are toward the righteous and his ears toward their cry. (Psalm 34:15)*

If you are a Christian, you have the great privilege of going to God with every need, every problem, every concern, every fear...and knowing that He hears and answers your prayer. But prayer is more than just asking for God's blessing—for God to do good to you. It is also praising Him, thanking Him, and telling Him that you

---

37 See 1 Kings 18 starting with verse 20.

sinned and asking for His forgiveness. Try to remember all these kinds of prayer when you pray to God.

Even though God does not always answer prayer the way we want Him to, He does always answer the prayers of His children. His answer is always right whether it is a "yes" answer, a "no" answer, or a "wait" answer, because God always does what is best for His children.

Pray

This week thank God for His attentiveness to His children and His promise to answer every prayer. Ask Him for the faith to believe that "No," and "Wait" answers are good answers. Pray that God would work in the heart of your children to believe that He is the one true God who always answers prayer, and whose answers are always right.

Promise: The Lord Will Guide You

Ask

If you were blindfolded and couldn't see where you were going, how could you walk from room to room without bumping into things?

Life will always be full of difficulties. Just as you would need to trust another person to guide you through the obstacles in your house, so we need God to guide us through the difficulties, problems, and decisions in life.

> *Trust in the LORD with all your heart, and do not lean on your own understanding. ⁶In all your ways acknowledge him, and he will make straight your paths. (Proverbs 3:5-6)*

Discuss

- What is the promise in this verse? What does "he will make straight your paths" mean? Does it mean you will never have problems? What does it mean?

- What are the conditions of this promise? What does it mean to trust in the LORD? Be specific.

- Give some examples of how we often lean on our own understanding.[38]

- Very practically, how can we acknowledge God in all our ways?

- Tell us about a time when you did not ask God for guidance and made a bad decision.

- Tell us about a time when you asked God for help to know what to do.

---

38 Make sure your children understand that we often forget to consult God, and we think we know what choice is right. We need to be humble enough to know we cannot trust our own wisdom. We need to seek God's help and ask Him to guide us.

Read

God has promised to guide His children. He instructs us through His Word and the godly counsel of others, and He watches over us with His "eye upon" us, ready to shepherd us back to His paths (Psalm 32:8). We are confronted in His Word with multiple examples of those who received God's counsel, walked in His ways, and experienced His blessing, as well as those who resisted God's counsel, walked in their own ways, and received His discipline. He leaves no doubt in His Word that following His ways is the path to blessing and joy.

It takes humility to trust in the Lord and to *not* lean on our own understanding, to continually acknowledge that we need His help and guidance. The human heart is prone to self-reliance, arrogance, and rebellion. We have the choice each day of either doing things *God's way* or *my way*. We have the choice of being gently led by the Lord as we consistently seek His counsel or being curbed with His discipline as a stubborn horse or mule is curbed with a bit and bridle.

This week, ask yourself if you are continually seeking the Lord's counsel, if you are truly trusting His wisdom and His heart for you, and if you are resisting Him in any way. Rejoice in God's sure promise that He will make straight your paths as you lean in dependence upon Him.

> *Trust in the LORD with all your heart, and do not lean on your own understanding. ⁶In all your ways acknowledge him, and he will make straight your paths. (Proverbs 3:5-6)*

For Younger Children: God has promised to guide His children—to show them what is right. He shows us His ways in the Bible and through the good advice of wise people. He also watches over us and leads us to what is right and good. The Bible tells us about many people who asked for God's help, walked in His ways, and were blessed. But we also read about people who did not listen to God, insisted on doing things their own way, and were disciplined. The Bible shows us that following God's ways is the way to great joy and goodness.

To trust in God and not in our own wisdom means we must be humble. We must admit that we need God's help every day, all day. Our own hearts want to do things our own way. But each day we can choose either to do things God's way or my way. We can either learn by God's gentle leading or by His discipline.

Ask God this week to show you if you are asking for His help and trusting His wisdom and goodness. Ask Him if you are being stubborn in any way. Thank God that, for His children, He promises to work all things out well when we depend on Him.

> *Trust in the LORD with all your heart, and do not lean on your own understanding. [6]In all your ways acknowledge him, and he will make straight your paths. (Proverbs 3:5-6)*

Pray

Pray for a humble dependence on God this week and for a submissive heart before Him. Ask the Lord to grant your children the wisdom to see the benefit of walking in God's ways and the folly of following their own way.

Promise: God Will Provide for Your Needs

Ask

What are some ways that birds get food? [39] Do you think birds worry about finding food?

The Bible tells us that God feeds the birds, and He clothes the flowers of the field (Matthew 6:26-29). If God takes care of birds and the flowers, how much more will He take care of His children?

> *And my God will supply every need of yours according to his riches in glory in Christ Jesus. (Philippians 4:19)*

Discuss

- What promise does God give His children in this verse? Does this verse promise that God will give you everything you want? Does it promise that God will give you everything you think you need? What exactly does it promise?[40]

- Can you think of examples of God providing for His children?

- Why is God able to provide for the needs of those who trust Him? What does "his riches in glory in Christ Jesus" mean?[41]

- How does this verse help us to fight worry?[42]

---

39 Birds eat bugs in trees, seeds in plants, crumbs people leave behind. Some birds eat worms, or they eat from bird feeders.

40 Make sure your children understand that by supplying our needs, God does not promise to make our lives comfortable but to give us what we need to persevere in faith. For example, He may not give us a bigger house, but He may give us the contentment and creativity we need to live in a smaller house.

41 God will provide from His abundance; God owns all things, so He has an unlimited supply to meet the needs of His children.

42 Additional reading: Matthew 6:25-34

- What kinds of things does God provide for you every day? Share a testimony of a unique way God provided for you or someone you know.

Read

How much time, energy, and emotion do you expend worrying about the cares of this world? How easy it is for us to forget the sure promise of God to care for His children. Yet He gives us daily reminders of His constant care—birds that neither sow nor reap, and yet are fed; flowers that don't spin or toil, and yet are beautifully clothed. God sends these reminders as reassurances that He cares for even the most insignificant. How much more is His care for His children?

Jesus' reminder to us in the Sermon on the Mount is to concern ourselves with seeking His Kingdom—striving to grow spiritually, to seek God, and to be a blessing to others. Then God's sure promise will be ours. He will supply every need of ours.

This is the promise of our faithful God to all those who trust in Jesus. Why do we worry when He possesses the goodness, power, and wisdom to fulfill this promise and all others? Surely, we can stand firm on His unshakable promise to care for us!

For Younger Children: We can spend a lot of time, energy, and emotion worrying about things. It is so easy for us to forget the sure promise that God will care for His children—even though God gives us reminders every day of His care. He shows us that He cares for birds. They don't grow crops, but God feeds them. Flowers don't sew clothing and yet they have beautiful petals to cover them. God sends us these reminders every day. If He cares for things like birds and flowers, won't He care for His children?

Jesus reminded us in the Sermon on the Mount to seek God's Kingdom. Instead of worrying about our daily needs, we should think about growing spiritually, trusting God, and being good to others. Then God's sure promise will be ours. He supplies every need of His children.

This is the promise of our faithful God to all who trust in Jesus. Why should we worry? God is full of goodness, power, and wisdom, and He can easily keep this promise and all His promises. Will you trust His promises?

Pray

This week, commit yourself to seeking God's Kingdom and rest in His sure promise to provide for His children. Pray that your children will have a greater desire to seek God than the things of this world.

Promise: God Will Not Withhold Any Good Thing

Ask

Can you think of something I would not let you have or do when you were younger? Why didn't I give you what you wanted?

God does not give us everything we want either...and He has a very good reason when He doesn't give us something.

> *For the LORD God is a sun and shield; the LORD bestows favor and honor. No good thing does he withhold from those who walk uprightly. (Psalm 84:11)*

Discuss

- What is this verse telling us about God by using the words "sun" and "shield"? What else does the first sentence tell us about God?[43]

- What is the promise in this verse? Who is it for? What does the word "withhold" mean? What does the word "no" in the phrase "no good thing" show us?

- If God does not withhold any good thing from His children, what does it mean then when God does withhold something?[44]

- Because we do not always understand God's ways and plans, what is the temptation we sometimes face when God does not give us what we ask? Explain. How can we fight that temptation?

---

43 God cares for His people, and He is a protector of His people. God is good and generous; He is kind to His children.

44 God will not withhold anything from His people that is good for them. If He withholds something, it is because it is not ultimately good for them. Note that the verse does not say that God will not withhold *anything from His children* but *no good thing.*

- How is God's definition (meaning) of "good" different from ours?[45]

- What are some examples of God's generosity toward you? (What good things has God given you or done for you?) Do you think more about the good that God has done for you or about what He has withheld from you?

Read

It is true that we want what we want…and when we don't get it, we aren't always very happy about it. But that shouldn't be the case because God has promised,

> For the LORD God is a sun and shield; the LORD bestows favor and honor. No good thing does he withhold from those who walk uprightly. (Psalm 84:11)

That is a very comprehensive promise. In fact, it couldn't be more comprehensive! *No good thing*—not even one! So we can have the assurance that anything that God withholds is not good for us. God is so very generous that He has given His very own precious Son. Any other thing would be a lesser thing to give.

He is so very wise that He knows what is good for us. And He loves us enough to *not* give us something that isn't good for us. Why should we not trust such a good and wise Father?

> He who did not spare his own Son but gave him up for us all, how will he not also with him graciously give us all things? (Romans 8:32)

For Younger Children: We want what we want. And when we don't get it, we aren't always very happy about it. But that is not the right way to think or feel because God has given His children this promise:

---

45 Our definition of "good" is something we like, not necessarily something that is good for us. God's definition of a "good thing" is something that is good for us; not something that makes us more comfortable but something that makes us more like His Son. We are often interested in fun and comfort, but God is interested in our faith and godly character.

For the LORD God is a sun and shield; the LORD bestows favor and honor. No good thing does he withhold from those who walk uprightly. (Psalm 84:11)

This is a broad, sweeping promise covering all things. God will not withhold even *one thing* that is good for His children. *Everything* that is good for His children He will give them. So if God withholds—holds back or does not give us—something, you can know for sure that it is not good for us. God is so generous that He has given us what is most precious to Him. He has given us His very own precious Son to die on the cross for our sins. Anything else is not as precious as His Son and would be less to give us.

God is so wise that He always knows what is good for us. And He loves His children so much that He will not give us something that is not good for us. What reason could we possibly have to *not* trust such a good and wise Father? There is no reason. We can trust God to do what is best for us!

> *He who did not spare his own Son but gave him up for us all, how will he not also with him graciously give us all things? (Romans 8:32)*

Pray

Thank God this week for His unending generosity. Thank Him for not sparing His own Son. Ask Him for the faith to believe that He will not withhold any good thing from His children and the conviction to trust Him when He does withhold something. Pray that your children will see God as immensely generous.

Promise: God Will Fight for You

Ask

What is something that you are afraid of now or have been afraid of in the past? What makes you (or made you) feel safer? (What helped you?)[46]

Everyone is afraid at times, and God understands this. He has given His children a wonderful promise we can hold onto when we are afraid or facing problems.

God is our refuge and strength, a very present help in trouble. (Psalm 46:1)

Discuss

- What is a refuge? How is God a refuge for His children?

- What is the importance of the words "very present"?

- God is a refuge (place of safety) for Christians because God not only protects and strengthens His people; He also fights for His people. What are some instances in the Bible when God fought for His people? What do these stories tell you about God? What do they tell you about how we should respond to difficulties and trouble?

- What is something you need help with? What does trusting in God to help you and be your refuge look like in this situation?

---

46 This can be as simple as being afraid of the dark and taking comfort in a teddy bear or a special blanket; or it could be something faced as an older child, such as a bully, fear of death, fear of failing, fear of what others think, etc.

Read

What battles are you facing today? What fears do you have? What worries plague you? What threatens your faith? God's promise is that He will fight for you!

> *God is our refuge and strength, a very present help in trouble.*
> *(Psalm 46:1)*

A present help means He is always there for us. He is our refuge, our place of safety, and our strength in our weakness. What a wonderful promise it is for the children of God that He will fight for us!

His unseen army surrounds us daily. If He would open our eyes to see His power and protection, we would face our daily battles with confidence. Like Gideon,[47] we would stand in amazement at His deliverance from all our troubles. It doesn't matter that we feel like an army of 300 against thousands—God is on our side!

> *From of old no one has heard or perceived by the ear, no eye has*
> *seen a God besides you, who acts for those who wait for him.*
> *(Isaiah 64:4)*

Rejoice in this promise this week and confidently say, "The Lord is my helper; I will not fear; what can man do to me?" (Hebrews 13:6).

For Younger Children: What problems or troubles do you have? What are you afraid of? What worries you? If you are a child of God, He promises to fight for you!

> *God is our refuge and strength, a very present help in trouble.*
> *(Psalm 46:1)*

A present help means He is always there for us. He is never absent. He is our refuge, our place of safety, and our strength in our weakness. God's wonderful promise to His children is that He will fight for us!

God's unseen army of angels surrounds us every day. If our eyes were opened like Elisha's servant's eyes were opened, we would

---

47 Judges 7:1-23

see God's army defending us.[48] If we could see His power and protection, we would face our daily battles knowing that God is fighting for His children. We would be amazed at how God helps His children in our troubles. Even though we cannot see God's army, we can have faith that God is our refuge, and He fights for His children. It doesn't matter that we may feel very small and weak. God is strong and He is on our side.

> *From of old no one has heard or perceived by the ear, no eye has seen a God besides you, who acts for those who wait for him. (Isaiah 64:4)*

What a wonderful promise this is! God is at work helping His children. If you truly believe that God is a refuge for His people and have the faith to trust Him, you can say with confidence, "The Lord is my helper; I will not fear; what can man do to me?" (Hebrews 13:6).

Pray

Pray for a heart of faith and confidence in God's strength and His care for you. Thank Him that He is a present help, and that He acts on behalf of His children. Pray that your children will trust in God as their refuge and strength, and that He will fight the enemy of their souls.

---

48 2 Kings 6:15-18

Promise: God Is Slow to Anger

Ask

What kinds of things make you angry?

God gets angry, too. But He never gets out-of-control angry. This is how the Bible describes God.

> *But you, O Lord, are a God merciful and gracious, slow to anger and abounding in steadfast love and faithfulness. (Psalm 86:15)*

Discuss

- How does this verse describe God? What does merciful and gracious mean?

- What does "slow to anger" mean? Does it mean that God never gets angry? Can you think of times in Bible when God was angry? Why was God angry? Was that God's first response?

- What does the word "abounding" mean? What does "abounding in steadfast love and faithfulness" mean? What are some examples of God's patience with and compassion on His people? What does this tell you about God?

- The Bible tells us that God "remembers that we are dust" (Psalm 103:14). What does this mean?[49] What does this show you about God's compassion on us? How would our lives be different if God were not slow to anger?

- How does God show His mercy, grace, patience, love, and faithfulness to you? How have you seen His slowness to anger

---

49 God created man from the dust of the ground (Genesis 2:7). The point of referring to the creation of man in Psalm 103 is to remind us that we are weak and dependent on God.

this week? In what ways have you needed God's kindness and patience this week?

Read

Our weaknesses are obvious to us. We have fears, worries, limitations, and sinful responses, and these often are the occasion for other people to get angry or lose patience with us. But God's response is so different from our sinful human response. He responds with patience and is slow to anger. He doesn't vent in frustration but responds with steadfast love. He remembers that we are "dust."

Though God would be justified to repay us according to our sin, He doesn't! His heart is always to forgive, restore, strengthen, and help. What an amazing God of steadfast love we have!

Through the example of God's patience with Moses, who was filled with fear at the thought of confronting Pharaoh and responded with great reluctance, we can see the patient, compassionate grace that God extends to His children. Jesus' example of love and forgiveness to those who crucified Him is a window into the heart of God.

We need not cower before God in our weakness, but rather rejoice that He knows that we are weak and loves us in spite of it. He is eager to help, support, encourage, and strengthen us, not to condemn us. Each day we should be amazed at the patience of God. How different our lives would be if God were not slow to anger. This is undeserved grace. What a precious promise to His children is God's promise to be slow to anger.

For Younger Children: We are all very weak. We have fears and worries. We are limited and sinful. So people sometimes become impatient or angry with us. But God is very different toward us than people are. He is patient and slow to anger. He doesn't get frustrated and strike out at us. He knows we are "dust," and He has great patience with our weaknesses.

It is very right for God to treat us as sinners who do not deserve His mercy. But He doesn't! God's heart is always ready to forgive, welcome us, strengthen us, and help us. God's steadfast love is amazing!

God treated Moses patiently when he was afraid to speak to Pharaoh. Jesus treated those who crucified Him with love and forgiveness. This shows us what kind of God we have. We do not need to be afraid of Him. God is patient and loving toward His children in our weakness. He is always ready and willing to help us, encourage us, and strengthen us rather than strike out at us in impatient anger.

Every day we should be amazed at the patience of God. Things for us would be so different if God were not slow to anger. We do not deserve His mercy and kindness. God's promise to be slow to anger is a very precious promise to His children.

Pray

This week, thank God for His patience with you. Ask Him to help you as you confront your weaknesses. Pray that your children will see the patient, compassionate heart of God through this verse and in their daily lives.

Promise: God Will Give You Strength

Ask

What are some reasons that soldiers give up in battle?[50]

We are in a battle, too, a spiritual battle. There are times when we are tempted to give up—to stop following Jesus, to quit doing what is right, to do things our own way. But God has given His children a wonderful promise.

> *"For the eyes of the LORD run to and fro throughout the whole earth, to give strong support to those whose heart is blameless toward him." (2 Chronicles 16:9a)*

Discuss

- What do the words "run to and fro throughout the whole earth" tell you about God?[51]

- What is the condition of this promise? Does a blameless heart mean a sinless heart? Who are those whose hearts are blameless toward God?

- We all have weaknesses. Think of areas in which you are weak, or think of a struggle that you have. It may be a habit or sin you are trying to overcome (e.g., procrastinating—putting things off instead of doing it; not telling the truth or stretching the truth; selfishness; worry). How can you look to God to give you strong support? Be specific.

---

50 The enemy is stronger than they are. They are tired of fighting. Too many of their fellow soldiers have been wounded or killed, and they feel alone in the battle. They run out of ammunition, they don't really believe in what they are fighting for, etc.

51 Make sure your children understand that God is not idly sitting by as life on earth goes on. He is actively involved in our daily lives. He is diligently looking and acutely aware of the needs of His children and eager to help them.

- What are some ways God can give you support?[52]

Read

What a wonderful thought it is that God's eyes run to and fro throughout the earth for the purpose of giving strong support to His children. Because we feel our weaknesses so acutely, the thought that God actively is pursuing our good, eager to strengthen us, is amazing. This should give us the confidence to face our fears, worries, and troubles. We have the almighty God, our Father, looking out for us, eager to help us, and willing to give His strong support to us.

Just as plaster of paris powder gains strength as it is united with water, so we gain strength when we are united with Christ. Alone, we are frail, but with Him, we are strong. This is a wonderful promise to dwell on this week as you depend on God so that you can "mount up with wings like eagles," and "run and not be weary," and "walk and not faint" (Isaiah 40:31).

For Younger Children: It is a wonderful thought that God is looking for ways to strengthen His people! He is not asleep or ignoring us. He is always watching and ready to help. We are weak in so many ways, but it is amazing that God wants to help His children! Remembering this can help you when you are afraid or worried, or when you have problems. Turn to God and ask for His help.

We are not strong on our own. But God is all-powerful. So, when God helps us, we are strong because of the strength He gives us. This week think about the wonderful promise that God will give His children strength. Depend on God so that you can "mount up with wings like eagles," "run and not be weary," and "walk and not faint" (Isaiah 40:31).

---

52 Make sure that your children understand that God's support is not only the personal confidence, peace, or resolve He gives you, but also the things He brings around you to help you—the support of others, verses or stories from His Word, sermons you have heard, the potential consequences He impresses on you or you are made aware of, etc.

Pray

Pray that you will walk in dependency on God this week. Ask Him to help your children to feel their weakness and believe that His strength can be theirs.

Promise: Though You Stumble, You Will Not Fall

Ask

Think about a time when you fell. What happened?

Though some falls can be quite serious, most of them are not. We may have a skinned knee or a bruised leg. But there is another kind of falling that the Bible talks about, a very serious kind of falling.

> *The steps of a man are established by the LORD, when he delights in his way; [24]though he fall, he shall not be cast headlong, for the LORD upholds his hand. (Psalm 37:23-24)*

Discuss

- What kind of falling does this verse mean?[53]

- What is the promise in this verse? What does it mean to be "cast headlong."[54]

- Who is this promise for?[55]

- What are some ways that God upholds the hands of His children when they stumble?

- How has God protected you from serious, continuing sin?

---

53 This is spiritual falling—sin. It can be lying, being unkind, doubting in the goodness of God and in His promises, worrying, refusing to do something God asks you to do, or some other sin. Spiritual falling is *for a moment*. This is not a long, rebellious, continuing of sin, but just a short moment of sinful behavior or attitude—a stumble. Make sure your children understand the difference between short sinful behavior repented of and deliberate, continual rebellion against God. Even people who love God sin sometimes, but they repent of their sin and turn away from it; they don't keep on sinning and continuing in their sin.

54 This is to be condemned due to continual, unrepentant sin.

55 It is for those who delight in God's ways, those who want to please God by following and obeying Him.

Read

The hold that sin can have on the heart and mind can be a frightening thing. Every true Christian battles sin daily. With God's help there is victory. But there are times when even sincere Christians fall. What keeps us from continuing down the path of destruction? God's promise does—His promise that "though he fall, he shall not be cast headlong, for the LORD upholds his hand." God has pledged to rescue His children from a path of continual unrepentant sin. What a joy and great relief it is to know that our steps are established by the LORD and that He upholds us.

Pondering the life of David should keep us from smug pride, though. Here was a man who followed God with all his heart, whose heart was wholly devoted to God, a man after God's own heart.[56] And yet his life was stained by horrific sin—adultery and murder. What would our response to David have been? Amazing grace flowed from the heart of his God! God sent Nathan to rebuke him and rescue him from continuing on a path of destruction that would lead to rejecting God and to eternal torment.

Surely, God is a covenant-keeping God who honors every one of His promises, including His promise to rescue us when we fall so that we will not be cast headlong. Though sin leaves its nasty scars, and the consequences of sin are never worth the fleeting pleasure of sin, God's rescuing grace pulls us back to Him and away from our sin. Repentance is a gift that keeps us from walking away from our God.

For Younger Children: It is very scary to think about the power of sin on our hearts and minds. If you are a true child of God, you will fight sin every day. God will help you to get victory over sin. But there are times when even true Christians fall or sin. However, a true Christian does not *continue* down a path of destruction. God promises His children that "though he fall, he shall not be cast headlong, for the LORD upholds his hand." God will rescue His children from staying in sin and refusing to repent.

King David can be an example for you. He was a man who loved God and wanted to follow God. But he sinned greatly by taking

---

56 Acts 13:22

another man's wife and having the man killed! What do you think should have happened to David? God is true to His promise to keep His children from continuing in their sin. God sent a prophet named Nathan to point out David's sin to him. God used Nathan to rescue David and keep him from continuing on a path of destruction that would lead David to turning away from God and going to hell.

God keeps all His promises, including the promise to rescue His children when they fall. Sin will still bring consequences that are very unpleasant. But God is gracious and turns His children back to Him and away from our sin. Repentance is a wonderful gift that keeps us from walking away from God.

Pray

This week, examine your heart. Is there any momentary sin there that you need to repent of? Thank God for His promise to uphold you and rescue you from your own heart. Pray that your children will be sobered by sin, rejoice in God's rescue, and ponder their spiritual standing before God.

Promise: God Will Discipline You

Ask

Think about a time when you were disciplined. What did you do? Why did your mother/father/teacher/boss discipline you? Why did this person discipline you? How did you feel about it? How did it help you? How do you feel about it now?[57]

God also disciplines His children.

> *My son, do not despise the LORD's discipline or be weary of his reproof, [12]for the LORD reproves him whom he loves, as a father the son in whom he delights. (Proverbs 3:11-12)*

Discuss

- What does "despise" mean? What should our attitude be toward discipline?

- Why do your parents discipline you? Why does God discipline His children?[58]

- What are some ways God disciplined Israel?

- How is God's discipline merciful (kind)?

- What is your attitude toward discipline? What changes do you need to make in your thinking? In your actions? In your attitudes?

---

57 Parents, you may want to share about a time when you were disciplined. Include the reason and the outcome.
58 Remind your children of the last devotional. God disciplines us to keep us from being cast headlong. God disciplines in love. He disciplines us for our good—to make us more like Jesus, to cause us to repent (Hebrews 12:10-11), to keep us from evil and great sorrow, to heal our sinful hearts, etc.

Read

God's ways are good and right and bring great blessing to those who walk in them. It is the desire of God's heart to bring the greatest blessing into the lives of His children. So when they swerve to the right or the left, He disciplines them to keep them walking in His good ways.

Just as good fathers discipline their children for their children's good, so God disciplines His children for the same reason. All of His discipline comes from a heart of love. He disciplines to cause repentance, to turn His children back to Him—never for revenge, but only in love. Though His discipline can be painful, He never disciplines more than is necessary, and His discipline is permeated with mercy. This is why Hosea declares:

> *"Come, let us return to the LORD; for he has torn us, that he may heal us; he has struck us down, and he will bind us up." (Hosea 6:1)*

What a wonderful promise it is that God will discipline us. He will not let us rebelliously make a destruction of our lives, but in love He will correct us. This is a blessing for which we should be extremely grateful. We need discipline because our hearts are prone to wander. But, like a good shepherd, God our Shepherd, lovingly disciplines us, bringing our hearts back to loving what is good and right. Is it no wonder then that the book of Proverbs tells us:

> *My son, do not despise the LORD's discipline or be weary of his reproof, [12]for the LORD reproves him whom he loves, as a father the son in whom he delights. (Proverbs 3:11-12)*

How often do we see discipline as a gift? How often do we thank God for it? May this devotional center our hearts on the goodness of God, the blessing of discipline, and the delight in walking in His ways.

For Younger Children: God's ways are always good and right. Following them brings blessing. God wants true joy for His children, So, when we turn toward sin, He keeps us walking in His good ways.

Just as good fathers discipline their children for their children's good, so God disciplines His children for our good. He always disciplines in love. He disciplines His children to cause repentance and turn us back to following Him and walking in His good ways. Discipline is painful, but God never disciplines more than is needed. His discipline is always full of love and mercy. This is why the prophet Hosea wrote:

> *"Come, let us return to the LORD; for he has torn us, that he may heal us; he has struck us down, and he will bind us up." (Hosea 6:1)*

It is a wonderful promise from God that He will discipline us. He will not let His children continue in rebellion and destroy our lives. Instead, He lovingly disciplines us. This is a wonderful gift that we should be thankful for. We need discipline from God and from our parents because our hearts are too often willing to sin. But God brings our hearts back to loving what is good and right. This is why the book of Proverbs tells us:

> *My son, do not despise the LORD's discipline or be weary of his reproof, [12] for the LORD reproves him whom he loves, as a father the son in whom he delights. (Proverbs 3:11-12)*

Do you see discipline as a gift? Do you thank God for it? Think about the goodness of God, the blessing of discipline, and the joy of walking in His ways.

Pray

Pray that you will have the correct attitude toward God's discipline, and that you will quickly repent when disciplined. Thank God for His shepherd's heart that lovingly keeps His children from straying too far from Him. Ask Him to help your children see that discipline is good and comes from love. Pray that He will give them a desire to walk in God's ways and center their hearts on Him.

Promise: God Plans Good for You

Ask

What good things happened to you today or this week? Explain how God's hand was in everything good that happened to you.[59]

God has made a special promise to do good to His children, a promise that He will not break.

> *"For I know the plans I have for you, declares the LORD, plans for wholeness and not for evil, to give you a future and a hope."* (Jeremiah 29:11, ESV 2003)

Discuss

- What is the significance of God having plans for our lives?[60]

- In your own words, what is the promise God gives His children in this verse?

- Does this mean that nothing bad will happen to Christians? Explain.[61]

- How does this verse help you look at things that happen with faith and hope?

- Is there something in your life you need to trust God with? (What are you concerned about? What possible good can you imagine could come from your struggles?)

- What can you thank God for?

---

59 See James 1:17.
60 Make sure your children understand that things don't happen randomly, but God has planned out each day of our lives. (See Psalm 139:1-16.) God does not *react to things; God is the initiator of good in our lives.*
61 Make sure your children understand that good does not mean easy or free from suffering or troubles. Everything that happens to believers will ultimately be turned for their good (Romans 8:28). God is more interested in our character, our holiness, than He is in our comfort (though He does much to make us comfortable). Good means what is good for us. God does nothing with evil intent but only with love.

Read

In the ups and downs of life, it is good to keep in perspective that God plans good for His children. He has a hopeful future for each of us, and His plans are for "wholeness and not for evil." To know that God is committed to our good should be a fear and worry eraser. We have the assurance that He has good in store for us.

Yet how easy it is to get into a complaining mode and to miss the mercies that are new every morning. Discontentedness is part of our fallen nature. But, as new creatures in Christ, we can live with a thankful heart, knowing that not only are there new mercies every day, but there is also a long-term good that God has in His plans for us. Hold on to this hope this week as you think about this devotional and navigate the ups and downs that this week holds.

For Younger Children: We all have good days and bad days. It is good to remind ourselves that God plans good for His children. If you are a child of God, tomorrow, the next day, and all the days of your life God's promise to you is to turn all things to good for you. What a wonderful promise this is! This promise can help us fight fear and worry. We have the promise that God plans good for us!

But we can easily become complainers and miss the mercies, the good things that God gives each day. Grumbling and complaining is part of our sin nature. But if you are a *new creature in Christ*— if you are trusting in Jesus as your Savior, you can live with a thankful heart. We can be thankful because, not only are there new mercies every day, but there is a wonderful plan that God has for our lives that is good for us. What a good promise to remember this week!

Pray

Pray that God will give you a thankful heart and help you to repent of any ingratitude or complaining spirit. Ask God to give your children eyes to see the goodness He lavishes on them each day and to desire the good plan He has for His children.

Promise: God Will Be With You in the Hard Times

Ask

Can you think of a long trip you took? What was at the end of that long trip? Was that end worth the long ride?

In this life, we will have times of difficulty. They may not seem to have a purpose, but God has good in them for us. And He makes a promise to His children for when we go through hard times.

> *When you pass through the waters, I will be with you; and through the rivers, they shall not overwhelm you... (Isaiah 43:2a)*

Discuss

- When this verse talks about waters and rivers, what does it mean?

- Does this verse promise Christians that they will not have troubles?[62] What does it promise?

- Why is it such a comfort that God will be with us in hard times? What do you know about God that makes this promise so precious?

- What kinds of things do we learn through problems and difficulties?[63]

---

62 See Psalm 34:19.
63 Make sure your children understand that difficulties teach us things that we would not otherwise learn. Suffering and problems help our faith grow strong. They help us to trust God and His promises. Difficulties teach us things like perseverance, contentment, gratitude, dependency on God, etc. A simple illustration is the difficulty of learning to ride a two-wheel bike, and the joy that came after that difficulty.

- What have you learned through hard times or a problem you had? How was God with you in the time of trouble?[64]

- What kinds of problems do you or your family have? Can you see how this could come from a loving God? Explain.

Read

We are no strangers to troubles. They come in all sizes, shapes, and levels of intensity. This is a fact of life, and Christians are not shielded from difficulty. On the contrary, the Bible says that "Many are the afflictions of the righteous" (Psalm 34:19a). We will pass through waters—many waters of hardship and suffering.

God allows His children to go through difficulty in order to build our faith—to make our confidence in Him and His promises strong, to learn lessons we need to learn, and to build the character of Christ in us. Though this is not easy, it is good for us, and it is part of God's promise to do good for us.

But, along with the *waters* of hardship and the many afflictions in this world, God makes a wonderful, comforting promise: "I will be with you." Just as God was with Stephen when he was being stoned,[65] giving him courage, strength, and peace, so He is with us in affliction. God's deliverance is not always a change in our circumstances; often it is His presence in the midst of difficulty, giving us all we need to endure trials victoriously.

May you find the sweet presence of God to be comforting in your difficulties and trials through life as you press on toward the reward of enjoying Him forever in heaven.

For Younger Children: Everyone has times of troubles. Sometimes they are big troubles, and sometimes they are little troubles. If you are a Christian, it does not mean that you will not have difficulties. Christians will "pass through the waters"—we will have suffering and hard times.

---

64 You may want to share a personal testimony with your children of how God was with you during a difficulty.
65 Acts 7:55-56

But this does not mean that God does not love us. God always loves His children. He lets us go through hard things so we will learn to trust Him and His promises, to learn lessons we need to learn, and to become more like Jesus. Times of trouble are not easy, but they are good for us.

But that is not the whole story. The really important thing is that God gives His children a wonderful promise about the hard times—He will be with us! He will help us, comfort us, encourage us, and care for us. Do you remember what happened to Stephen when he was stoned? God gave him courage, strength, and peace. God helped Stephen in time of trouble.

God does not always take away the trouble, but He will give us all we need to get through the hard times. Look to God when times are hard and keep trusting Him. Someday His children will have the wonderful reward of enjoying God forever in heaven.

Pray

Pray this week that you will sense the presence and help of God throughout your day, and that He will give you a right perspective of suffering. Ask Him to help your children to see that the trials of the Christian life are minor compared to the joy of heaven.

Promise: God Will Not Bring Any Unnecessary Suffering into Your Life

Ask

(Ask your children why something unpleasant is necessary. Make this something pertinent to your child's life. For example: "Why is it necessary to do finger exercises/play scales on the piano when all you want to do is play the piano? Why is it necessary to run laps when you just want to play basketball? Why is it necessary to take math in school even though you don't like it? Why do we make you take out the garbage and empty the dishwasher?" The point you are trying to get at is that some unpleasant things are necessary now for a better outcome later.)

God knows that unpleasant things are necessary. Let's read what God's Word tells us about the suffering God brings into our lives.

> *but, though he cause grief, he will have compassion according to the abundance of his steadfast love;* [33] *for he does not afflict from his heart or grieve the children of men. (Lamentations 3:32-33)*

Discuss

- What does it mean that God *causes grief*?

- What does this verse show you about God's heart?

- If God is loving and compassionate, then why does He cause grief or bring suffering into our lives?

- Have your parents or your teachers ever caused you to *suffer*? Why?

- Can you think of a situation where you went through something painful but later realized it was for your good? Did someone cause the suffering? What was the reason they did this? (You may want to share an example with your children.)

- How do the difficulties we go through in life teach us to trust God?

- Are you struggling with anything difficult now? How can we pray for you? How can we help you?

Read

Lazarus was a close friend of Jesus, as were Lazarus' two sisters, Mary and Martha. Yet when Lazarus was dying and the sisters sent for Jesus, the Great Physician delayed two days in coming—until Lazarus was dead. The scene that greeted Jesus was one of mourning, for by that time Lazarus had been in the tomb for four days.[66] *Why didn't Jesus come sooner? Why didn't He heal Lazarus?*

It was because Jesus had a better plan. The suffering He caused was necessary—necessary to the faith of those who would see Jesus raise Lazarus from the dead and believe as they beheld the glory of God. Surely, a few days of grieving was worth an eternity of joy for those who believed.

God causes suffering—but only the suffering necessary to do what is best for His children. He loves us enough to weep with us as we go through trials—and enough to allow the trial to do its good work in us and for us. Far from being oblivious or callous to our pain, God understands the pain of His children. He is full of compassion and, in His abundance of steadfast love, He does not willingly afflict or grieve us.

Yet He knows that suffering is a necessary teacher for our stubborn and blind souls. This is why He humbled proud King Nebuchadnezzar after warning him to repent. Only after losing his faculties and behaving like a wild animal, did Nebuchadnezzar repent and acknowledge God's greatness.[67] The resulting praise is a testimony to the value of suffering and the compassionate reason our loving

---

66 John 11:1-44
67 Daniel 4:29-37

God causes affliction. May we, in our hardest moments, affirm that God weeps with us and does not willingly afflict or grieve us. We have a compassionate Father whose steadfast love is abundant.

For Younger Children: Lazarus and his sisters Mary and Martha were good friends of Jesus. But when Lazarus was dying and the sisters sent for Jesus to help Lazarus, Jesus didn't come right away. Jesus waited until Lazarus died. Then He came and saw everyone weeping at the tomb where Lazarus was buried. *Why didn't Jesus come sooner and heal Lazarus? Didn't Jesus care about His friends?*

Yes, Jesus cared very much! And He had a better plan for His friends and their friends, and for us! He loved them so much that He wanted to give them a strong faith. Lazarus had to die so that Jesus could bring him back to life. Now they would truly understand that Jesus is God. Now they would truly understand the power of God!

God causes suffering, but He only causes what is needed to do what is best for His children. He loves us enough to weep with us as we go through hard things. He lets those hard things teach us and change us. God knows about every sad or hard thing His children go through. He understands our pain and weeps with us. He is not happy that we have to suffer sometimes, but He knows that sometimes it is good for us. God is always kind and loving and always does what is best for us.

Pray

What difficulties do you struggle with? Can you thank God for them recognizing that only necessary suffering comes to you? Thank God for His abundant love and compassion for you. Pray that your children will understand that God grieves over the suffering of man, and yet loves man enough to cause necessary suffering for our good.

Promise: If You Remain Steadfast Under Trial, You Will Be Rewarded

Ask

Do you remember learning to [ride a bicycle/skate/ice skate/play an instrument]? [68] *Was it hard at first? What was hard about it? Are you glad you kept trying? Why?*

The Bible tells us about a much greater reward than the reward of learning [to ride a bike/ice skate/play an instrument].

> *Blessed is the man who remains steadfast under trial, for when he has stood the test he will receive the crown of life, which God has promised to those who love him. (James 1:12)*

Discuss

- What does "blessed" mean? [69]

- What does "steadfast" mean in this verse?

- What is the "crown of life"? [70]

- What are some ways to "remain steadfast" in trials? (What are some practical ways to fight the fight of faith?)

- How did Jesus remain steadfast on the cross? (See Hebrews 12:1-2.) What helped Jesus endure His suffering? How does this verse prove that James 1:12 is true?

- Is there anyone you know who is experiencing a difficult trial? How can we help that person?

---

68 Note something that your children have learned to do that was at first hard but brought the reward of now doing that thing and receiving joy from it.
69 It means happy, having the favor of God, which brings a deep, joy-filled contentment.
70 It is the eternal life that comes through salvation.

Read

We all have problems—some big and some little. But each one can either be a threat to our faith or an opportunity to build spiritual muscle. Rather than entertain the lies of the enemy and doubt God's goodness, God has given us an incentive to remain steadfast. Looking to the promised reward of eternal life—focusing on the future blessing rather than the present circumstances—can provide the determination to remain steadfast. The trials we face here are so insignificant compared to the glory to come! Stand stubbornly unmovable in the face of difficulties because the crown of life is our promised reward!

Just as the Apostle Paul did not have the strength to endure suffering alone, neither do we. Our weakness is very real. But God doesn't ask us to stand alone. He offers His strength in our weakness. The grace He provides when we are tempted to give up and give in to discouragement or unbelief will keep us standing firm. He is our sufficiency when we depend on Him.

For Younger Children: Everyone has problems. Some problems are big, and some are small. Each problem can either make our faith in God stronger or weaker. Satan wants us to believe his lies— lies like, "God doesn't love you. He doesn't care about you and your problem. God is not good. God can't help you." Do not believe Satan's lies! Instead, believe God's Word! We will receive a wonderful reward if we trust in God. Someday we will have a really wonderful life in heaven!

God knows that we are weak, and it is hard to stand strong in faith. So ask Him for His help. He will help those who ask Him.

Pray

Pray that God will give you a heavenly perspective in the face of difficulties this week, a joy in anticipating the promised reward to His children, and His strength in your weakness. Ask God to give your children an understanding of their weakness and their need for Him. Pray that they would have a holy imagination that would draw their hearts to desire a heavenly inheritance.

Promise: The Lord Will Keep You from Harm

Ask

Do Christians ever get hurt or sick? What do you think it means that God promises to keep His children from harm?

Timothy helps us to answer this question:

> *The Lord will rescue me from every evil deed and bring me safely into his heavenly kingdom. To him be the glory forever and ever. Amen. (2 Timothy 4:18)*

Discuss

- If this verse does not mean that Christians will not suffer, what kind of protection or rescue is God promising in this verse?[71]

- Does this mean that Christians will never have doubts or spiritual struggles? Explain.

- What other promise does God give His children in this verse?[72] How does this promise help us today?

- Since God will safely bring His children to heaven, does that mean that we don't have to fight for our faith? Explain.[73]

- How can you fight for your faith? (Be specific.)

---

71 Make sure your children understand that God protects the faith of His children. He rescues us from ultimate harm to our souls and the evil that Satan plots against us to cause us to turn away from God. God will keep His children from ultimate harm to their souls.

72 God promises to guide us safely through the pitfalls of unbelief so that we inherit eternal life in heaven.

73 One of the means God uses to protect our faith is to give us the will to fight the fight of faith. So our efforts are fueled by God's grace, but we still need to strive to believe and grow in faith.

Read

Promises like *the Lord will keep you from harm* are sometimes hard to understand in the context of real life. Does it mean that no harm will ever come to a Christian? Christians won't suffer hurt, sickness, or persecution? Though we understand that this is not what this promise means, it may be harder for your children to understand this.

The reassurance you can give children is that God has promised to protect the faith of His children, and no ultimate harm will come to their souls. He has given His children the shield of faith to protect them against the fiery darts of the evil one.[74]

Shadrach, Meshach, and Abednego stood firm in face of the threats to bodily harm, as their confidence in God was strong. Their faith was solid, and they responded with bold confidence in the power and goodness of God. We, too, can have that same confidence in the face of harm.

For Younger Children: It is a little hard to understand the promise that *the Lord will keep you from harm.* We know that Christians get hurt, sick, and sometimes treated badly. So what does this promise mean?

The wonderful meaning of this promise is that God has promised to protect the faith of His children. No lasting harm will come to their souls—they will not permanently turn away from God. God gives His children faith to protect them from Satan's attacks.

Do you remember the story in the Bible of Shadrach, Meshach, and Abednego?[75] They stood strong in faith even though they were thrown in the fiery furnace. God protected their faith! And He also protected their lives. No matter what happens to a true child of God, we know that no one can take away our faith. We can stand strong knowing we have the promise that God will bring us to heaven with Him some day.

---

74 Ephesians 6:11-17
75 Daniel 3:8-30

Pray

Pray this week that you will recognize the fiery darts of the evil one, and boldly and confidently take up the shield of faith. Ask God to give your children confidence in His power and goodness.

Promise: God Will Deliver You from All Your Troubles

Ask

Suppose you need $5. Your grandmother promises to help you get the $5. Her neighbor needs someone to weed her garden and will pay $5 for the help. Your grandmother will recommend you to her neighbor. You may not like the way your grandmother keeps the promise. But is this a real promise that you can count on?

We can always count on God's promises, too, though we may not understand how God keeps His promises. Let's talk about the promise in Psalm 34:17.

> *When the righteous cry for help, the LORD hears and delivers them out of all their troubles. (Psalm 34:17)*

Discuss

- What is the promise in this verse?

- What is the condition?

- There are different ways God delivers His children from trouble. What are some ways God delivers Christians?[76]

- Why does God have the right to determine how to deliver His children from trouble? Do we need to be concerned about the way God will deliver us? Why?[77]

- Do you have any troubles we can pray about?

---

76 Make sure your children understand that God can take the trouble away, He can give the grace to endure the trouble, or He can deliver us through death.
77 Make sure your children understand that God's deliverance is sure and that He knows what is best for us. So His way of deliverance is good for us (Roman 8:28).

Read

Surely, the story of God's rescue of Shadrach, Meshach, and Abednego from the fiery furnace is one of the most reassuring stories of God's care for His children in the Old Testament.[78] We would love for God to rescue us from every one of our troubles in such a decisive and dramatic manner.

But God reserves the right to deliver His children from their troubles in His own way and His own time. Sometimes He does perform a dramatic rescue. Sometimes He delivers us by giving us the grace to endure the trouble. And sometimes He delivers us when He brings us to heaven. Whatever His deliverance looks like, it is the result of His faithfulness to keep His promise to deliver His children from trouble when they call to Him for help.

Let us rejoice in the greatest deliverance He has given His children—the deliverance from their greatest problem, the problem of sin and separation from Him. Regardless of what trouble Christians encounter on earth, our souls are secure in eternity. This truly is the greatest deliverance.

As we face trouble in this life, let us take hold of God's sure promise to deliver His children from trouble, and walk with faith and trust in His promise and the means by which He keeps it.

For Younger Children: The story of God rescuing Shadrach, Meshach, and Abednego from the fiery furnace is a great story! It shows us that God cares for His children. We would like it if God solved all our troubles in such a wonderful way.

But God doesn't always deliver His children the way we want Him to. God knows what we need most and the best way to help us. Sometimes He rescues us by taking our troubles away. But other times He gives us the grace and the strength to bravely go through the trouble. There are times that God's rescue comes when He brings us to heaven. No matter how God works, we know that He will be faithful to keep His promise to deliver His children when they call to Him for help.

---

78 Daniel 3:8-30

Do you know what is the greatest rescue God has given to His children? It is delivering us from our sin problem. The worst problem we have is our sin problem, and the greatest deliverance is the forgiveness for sin that Jesus paid for on the cross. If you are trusting Jesus as your Savior, remember that no matter what happens to you in this life, you will live forever with Jesus in heaven!

Pray

This week ask the Lord to give you faith and confidence in His promise to deliver His children from trouble. Pray that God will deliver your children from their greatest problem—the problem of sin and separation from Him.

Promise: Joy Comes with the Morning

Ask

What are some things that are really hard for you to wait for?

We don't really like to wait very long, but God gives His children a wonderful promise that helps us to wait.

> *Weeping may tarry for the night, but joy comes with the morning.*
> *(Psalm 30:5b)*

Discuss

- There are some very real sorrows in this world. What are some of them?

- What does this verse say about our sorrows?[79]

- What promise does this verse make?

- We don't know how long it will take for the *morning* to come, so what are some things we can do to encourage ourselves to wait with faith? (Think of specific strategies.)

- Is there someone we can pray for and ask God to give them strength until the morning comes?

Read

Sorrow is a very real and all too common experience in this broken world. The Bible makes no claim that Christians will not weep. We see it all through the Bible as God's people experience being sinned

---

79 Tarry means to remain, stay, or delay—a sorrowful situation may seem to last a long time.

against, and as their own sins cause sorrow. But the story of every true believer has a good end—joy comes with the morning.

Just as the sorrow of the disciples at the death of Jesus turned to joy at His resurrection, so someday Jesus will bury our sorrow and resurrect joy for us. In the middle of the sorrow, we don't see the end, but we must remember that the story isn't over yet. There is a happy ending for every believer.

> *Weeping may tarry for the night, but joy comes with the morning.*
> *(Psalm 30:5b)*

Sometimes the night is long, but the morning always comes for God's children. During the night, we are called to fight for joy by remembering God's promises, trusting His wisdom and goodness, and recognizing that we are in the middle of the story and God promises a good ending. Weeping is real. But it is only for the night. Take heart, Christian: The story isn't over yet. Joy comes with the morning!

For Younger Children: There are many sad things in this broken world. The Bible shows us that God's people will have troubles. But every Christian's story will have a very good ending—joy comes with the morning!

The disciples were very sad at the death of Jesus. But their sorrow turned to joy at His resurrection. That helps us to know that someday Jesus will bury our sorrow and give us new joy! In the middle of our sorrows, we don't see the end. But we can still remember that the story isn't over yet. For every child of God, there is a happy ending!

> *Weeping may tarry for the night, but joy comes with the*
> *morning. (Psalm 30:5b)*

Sometimes our sorrows last a long time. Sometimes the night is long, but the morning always comes for God's children. When things are hard, we must fight for joy by remembering God's promises, trusting His wisdom and goodness, and reminding ourselves that we are in the middle of the story that God promises has a good ending. Weeping is very real. But it is only for *the night*. If you are a child of God, the story isn't over yet. Joy comes with the morning!

Pray

Pray for the faith to believe in God's goodness and wisdom in the middle of things, and to fill your heart with the reassurance that joy comes with the morning. Pray that your children will see that God's plans and ways are both wise and good, that sorrow is necessary, and that for the Christian sorrow gives way to joy.

Promise: All Things Work Together for Good

Ask

What kinds of things do you worry about? What specifically are you concerned about?[80]

God has given His children a promise that, if we truly believe it with all our hearts, should lessen our worries.

> *And we know that for those who love God all things work together for good, for those who are called according to his purpose. (Romans 8:28)*

Discuss

- What is the condition of this promise?

- What specifically does God promise in this verse?

- What does this verse tell you about God?

- What does the term "work together" imply?[81]

- How do we define "good"? Look at Romans 8:29. How does God define "good"?

- Why should this promise help us with our worries and fears? Explain.

---

80 Everyone has some kind of worries. Your goal is to help your children identify what causes them to be fearful or anxious. What are the possible negative outcomes your children anticipate that are connected with this particular concern?

81 Help your children to realize that "work together" implies many moving parts. So the outcome may take time; it may not be immediate.

Read

One of the most reassuring promises in the Bible for the believer is Romans 8:28—that all things work together for our good, every single thing. Since everything is under God's control, nothing can happen to us that is not ordered by God and is not for our good.

Though we would like all things that happen to us to be pleasant things, the reality is that we often need the hard things in life. *Good* does not necessarily mean *pleasant*. Good means *good for us*—to conform us to the image of His Son. God is more interested in our character than in our comfort. The greatest good He can do for His children is to make them strong in faith. So the hard things work to build strong faith in believers...and are good for us.

Just as Naaman's leprosy was good for him and led him to faith in the one true God,[82] so God uses the circumstances in our lives to bless us. We have a faithful God who knows the means to build our faith and character, and who will never break His promise to order all things in our lives for our good. Praise Him for His goodness and His faithfulness!

For Younger Children: Romans 8:28 is a very comforting verse. It tells us that, if we are God's child, everything that happens to us will be for our good. God controls all things. So nothing can happen to His children except what God knows is good for us.

We would like everything in our lives to be happy and pleasant. But sometimes we need the hard things in life, too. *Good* doesn't mean fun or pleasant. Good means *good for us*. What is good for us is to be like Jesus. God wants His children to be strong in faith. That is more important to Him than making everything fun for us. Hard things can make us strong in faith...so they are good for us.

Do you remember Naaman in the Bible? He had a bad sickness called *leprosy*. God used Naaman's leprosy to show Naaman that the God of Israel is the one true God. God used Naaman's bad sickness to give him good faith. Just like God knew what Naaman

---

82 2 Kings 5:1-14

needed, He knows what we need. He uses everything in the lives of His children for our good. God is good and He is faithful.

Pray

This week, thank God for His sovereign control in your life and the reassuring promise that all things work for good for those who love God and are called according to His purpose. Pray that your children will understand God's goodness and desire to be a child of God.

Promise: God Will Not Forsake His People

Ask

Can you think of something you threw away? Why did you throw it away?

The Bible tells us about something that God will never throw away—for any reason.

> *For the LORD will not forsake his people; he will not abandon his heritage; (Psalm 94:14)*

Discuss

- What does the word "forsake" mean?[83]

- The word *abandon* means the same thing. "Heritage" in this sentence is the same as people. Why does this verse say the same thing two times?

- What does this verse tell you about God?

- Do God's children deserve His forever love? Why does God make this promise to His children?

- If God does not forsake His children, does that mean that Christians can sin as much as they want and it doesn't matter? What is wrong with this?

- How can you show faithful love to God?

---

83 It means to quit, to get rid of, to leave entirely, or to leave without intending to return, to completely turn away from. In this context, it means to turn away from someone, to leave someone behind, to forget about someone.

Read

How quickly we get tired of things and throw them away or get rid of them. This same attitude sometimes carries over into our relationships with people. When an acquaintance annoys or frustrates us, we often look for friendship in other places. We are quick to move on to other people who will be less bothersome, more encouraging, or more fun.

God is not like us. He loves His children with an everlasting love and promises to never forsake us—even though we do not deserve His faithful love. He is faithful in spite of our failings, never breaking His covenant of love. He has given us a beautiful picture of His covenant love in the life of Hosea, the prophet.[84] Hosea forgave his unfaithful wife, Gomer, reclaiming her from slavery, not to be his slave but to reinstate her as his wife.

How can anyone read the story of Hosea without marveling at the faithful love of this loyal husband and true follower of God? Yet Hosea was only a mere reflection, a shadow, of the kind of husband God is to His people. We, the bride of Christ, are loved with an everlasting love, and God will never break covenant with us. How amazing is it to be loved with such unfailing love—to know that we will never be forsaken? Truly, we have a great heritage as the people of God.

For Younger Children: We get tired of things very quickly. Then we throw them away or give them away. We can also treat people the same way. Sometimes when a friend does something we don't like, we stop being that person's friend. We look for other friends that we like better.

But God is not like us. He loves His children with a forever love. He promises never to leave us. We don't deserve God's love, but God is still faithful to His children. He never stops loving His children—even when we make mistakes or sin. What a wonderful promise God's children have that God will never leave them! God's love for His children is amazing!

---

84 Hosea 1

Pray

Thank God this week for His everlasting love. Confess your unfaithfulness to Him, and ask Him to make you a pure, spotless bride. Pray that your children will each long to be a child of God, and a recipient of not only His precious promises, but of His everlasting, covenant love.

Promise: God Will Not Forget His Promises

Ask

Can you think of a time when you didn't do something you said you would do?[85]

Do you know that God never forgets what He says? And He always does what He says He will do.

"...I am watching over my word to perform it."—Jeremiah 1:12b

Discuss

- What does it mean that God is "watching over" His Word?

- What does "perform it" mean?[86]

- In your own words, what is the promise in this verse?

- What does this verse tell you about God?

- What makes it hard for us to believe that God is working and will keep His promises?

Read

How often we misjudge God simply because we are not aware of what He is doing. God is always at work; He is watching over His Word to perform it. And yet His work is often hidden to us. This is where faith comes in. Will we trust Him even when things look wrong, or when it looks like He is not at work?

---

85 Parents: Be ready to provide an example of your own if your children can't think of one.
86 It means to do it.

This is the situation that Joseph was in. He had been given two prophetic dreams by God, and yet he found himself at the bottom of a pit.[87] Where was God? Where was the fulfillment of His plan, purposes, and promise? Joseph had two choices at that point. He could look down at himself and his situation and swim in a sea of self-pity, or he could look up to God in wonder and amazement at what He might be doing.

We have these same two choices every day. Will we look at our circumstances, difficulties, and unfulfilled dreams and feel that God has cheated us? Or will we, with the shield of faith, stand firm, trusting the almighty, sovereign, good God and Father of His children? This is the battle facing every Christian. May you walk in victory this week and demonstrate to others that they can put their confidence in God.

For Younger Children: Sometimes we think that God is not working to keep His promises because we don't know what He is doing. But God is always at work, even though we can't see it. That is why we need faith. We need faith to trust God even when things don't seem so good or when it looks like He has forgotten about us.

Do you remember the story in the Bible of Joseph? God gave him two dreams that someday he would rule over his family. But Joseph ended up in the bottom of a pit! That didn't seem right! Did God forget about Joseph? Joseph was supposed to rule, to be in charge. Joseph had two choices. He could look down at his situation and feel sorry for himself. Or he could look up to God and wonder with amazement at what God might be doing.

We have the same choice Joseph had. We can look at our situation, problems, and disappointments and think that God has forgotten about us. Or we can stand strong in faith trusting the all-powerful, always watching, always working, good God. We can fight for faith to believe that God will always do what He says He will do.

---

87 Genesis 37:1-24

Pray

Pray this week that you will have a heart of faith that looks up at the goodness and sovereignty of God, and faces each day free from complaining, worry, and self-pity. Ask God to open the eyes and the hearts of your children to see and trust that they can put their confidence in Him.

Look Up, Not Down

Ask

The Bible tells us a good way to look at problems or troubles.

For this light momentary affliction is preparing for us an eternal weight of glory beyond all comparison, [18]as we look not to the things that are seen but to the things that are unseen. For the things that are seen are transient, but the things that are unseen are eternal. (2 Corinthians 4:17-18)

Discuss

- Afflictions are problems or troubles. What does this verse tell us about the purpose of troubles?[88]

- What advice does this verse give us about how to think about our problems?[89]

- What does this verse show us about our view of time compared to God's view of time? Why is there a difference?

- When we are going through hard things, they don't seem light (easy) or momentary (short). Why is this?

- What can help you look ahead to the eternal things?

- What will help you trust God in times of trouble?

- Is there anything we can pray about for you?

---

88 They are preparing us for wonderful blessings in heaven; it is the forever favor of God on us; we will experience God's pleasure in us for enduring trials

89 Make sure your children understand that we need to focus on the hidden spiritual benefits of suffering—we need to look ahead to the eternal rewards

Read

As we progress through the history of Joseph's life, we see a series of setbacks.[90] Though he is a slave, God places him in a position of overseeing his master's household—until he is falsely accused and imprisoned. In prison, he is eventually given responsibility again as an overseer and sees hope in the release of Pharaoh's cupbearer, who can plead his innocence to Pharaoh. But he sits in prison two more years, having been forgotten by the cupbearer.

But he hadn't been forgotten by God—and neither are we when we go through setbacks and disappointed hopes. God is still on the throne orchestrating His perfect plan for us, His children. He promises that the "light momentary affliction is preparing for us an eternal weight of glory." The Bible instructs us then to look to the unseen things—the eternal things of spiritual battles being fought and won in our own hearts, and in the world around us.

May you, with joyful hope and anticipation of unseen eternal things, look up with confidence in the wisdom and love of your heavenly Father as you navigate the setbacks and even the ordinary challenges of your daily life. He is still on the throne keeping His promises!

For Younger Children: Joseph's life after being in the pit wasn't easy. He had more problems! He became a slave. God put Joseph in charge of his master's household—until the master's wife lied about Joseph. Then Joseph was put in prison! God gave Joseph favor in prison, and he was put in charge of some of the things in the prison. Joseph hoped one of Pharaoh's (the king's) servants would help him when the servant got out of jail. But Joseph sat in jail two more years.

However, God didn't forget about Joseph. And God hasn't forgotten about us when things don't seem to go well for us. God is working out His good and perfect plan for His children. He promises that the "light momentary affliction" will bring eternal joy. The Bible tells us to look at the faith battles being fought and won in our own hearts. Then we can look up to God

---

90 Genesis 39-40

with confidence in His wisdom and love. God is still keeping His promises to His children!

Pray

Pray that God will give you eyes to perceive the unseen battles around you and the faith to trust Him. Ask Him to help your children see the spiritual battle for their souls and place their confidence in God.

God Is Accomplishing His Purposes

Ask

What are some of your plans for the future? Is there anything that could change your plans or any reason why you might not be able to do what you have planned? Explain.

Nothing ever changes God's plans. He always does what He plans to do!

> *The LORD of hosts has sworn: "As I have planned, so shall it be, and as I have purposed, so shall it stand," (Isaiah 14:24)*

Discuss

- What is the promise God makes in this verse?

- Why can't anyone or anything stop God's plans?

- What do you know about God that gives you confidence that God can do what He says He will do?

- What promise of God can help you today?

Read

We left Joseph in prison, yet on the threshold of seeing the amazing purposes of God unfold in his life. God, in His astounding providence, purposed for Joseph to save His children from famine, preserving their lives and thus fulfilling God's promise to make of Abraham a great nation. All the events of Joseph's life fit together to move him toward this great purpose. From our perspective of seeing the whole story, we marvel at God's wisdom and goodness.

Yet what must have it have been like for Joseph serving in Potiphar's house and sitting in prison? His dreams were given to him as a young boy. At 17, he was sold into slavery. At 30,[91] he became the overseer of Egypt, and he was almost 40 when he saw the dream fulfilled.[92] What must that 23-year wait have been like for Joseph? Was it faith-filled, or did he question God's purposes and promises?

Surely, we have some hints in his declarations to his brothers that Joseph was keenly aware of God's purpose in his suffering. God had sent him to "preserve for you a remnant on earth, and to keep alive for you many survivors" (Genesis 45:7). He understood that his brothers were not in charge, but God sovereignly reigns—"So it was not you who sent me here, but God...As for you, you meant evil against me, but God meant it for good, to bring it about that many people should be kept alive" (Genesis 45:8; Genesis 50:20). What a biblical perspective he had on the work of God in his life. Surely, he would affirm the truth of Romans 8:28, that "all things work together for good" for the people of God. Oh, that we might also look beyond our microscopic view of ourselves to the great and glorious purposes of God!

For Younger Children: What happened to Joseph? Did he stay in prison? Pharaoh needed Joseph's help to understand a dream. When Joseph helped him, Pharaoh made Joseph second in charge of Egypt. Joseph became an important man in Egypt just as God had planned...and God planned this for a good reason! When there was no food in Israel, there was food in Egypt, and God used Joseph to save his family from starving.

All the things that happened in Joseph's life worked together to make him able to have this important job and to save God's children so that they could become a great nation. We can look back and see that God had a good and wise plan.

But Joseph didn't see the end of things when he was sold into slavery. He was almost 40 years old when he saw his dream come true. He did rule over his family. But he had to wait many

---

91 Genesis 41
92 Genesis 42-45

years for this to happen. That meant many years of trusting God's promise.

The Bible tells us that Joseph understood that God had good purposes in Joseph's suffering. God had sent him to Egypt to keep the Hebrew people alive. His brothers were not in charge when they sold him into slavery. God was in charge, and God sent Joseph to Egypt. The wrong that Joseph's brothers did, God used for good. Joseph understood this. It is true that "all things work together for good" for the people of God. Can you look beyond your own situation and trust in the great and glorious purposes of God?

Pray

Pray that God would give you a confidence in His purposes in your life, and that you would rest in His wisdom and goodness. Ask Him to give your children a desire to be a part of His Kingdom purposes and to glorify Him in their lives.

God Is Not Slow in Keeping His Promises

Ask

We see that Joseph had to wait a long time for God's promise to be fulfilled. What have you waited a long time for?

The Bible gives us a verse to help us while we are waiting for God to act.

> *I believe that I shall look upon the goodness of the LORD in the land of the living!* [14]*Wait for the LORD; be strong, and let your heart take courage; wait for the LORD! (Psalm 27:13-14)*

Discuss

- What is the psalmist saying in the first verse? (What is he confident of?)

- What is the psalmist's advice for us as we wait for God to work?

- Can you think of any instances in the Bible where someone had to wait for God to keep His promise? Why was waiting good for these people?

- Is there anything you are anxious about? What does trusting God with this situation look like?

Read

Waiting is always hard. It is hard when you are a little child waiting to open your Christmas presents, and it is hard when you are an adult waiting for God to fulfill His promise in your life. Yet God's people have often had to wait for God to act. Abraham waited for the promised heir, David waited to become king of Israel, Israel waited for the Messiah, and we are still waiting for the return of Jesus.

Sometimes it seems to us that God is slow—very slow to keep His promises. But the Bible tells us that He isn't slow. He has good reasons for delaying, and His timing is perfect. He knows things we are not aware of, and He has purposes far greater than our own.

As the people of God, we are called to wait in faith—trusting in God's goodness and wisdom, trusting that He will act at the right time, trusting that all things work for our good and His glory. May we not fall into the trap that Jacob fell into and take things into our own hands.[93] But may we wait patiently and with confidence for the Lord.

For Younger Children: Waiting is hard. Waiting until you can open your Christmas presents is hard. And waiting for God to keep His promises is hard, too. God's people have had to wait for God to act many times. Abraham waited to have the promised son, Isaac. David had to wait to become king of Israel. Israel waited for the Messiah. We are waiting for Jesus to return.

Sometimes it seems to us that God is very slow to keep His promises. But the Bible says God is not slow in keeping His promises. He has good reasons for what He is doing, and His timing is always perfect. He knows things we don't know about, and His plan is always better than ours.

God's children must wait in faith. We must trust God's goodness and wisdom. We must believe God knows just the right time to keep His promise. We must trust that all things work for good for His children. All things work to show He is a great God, too. God's children must be careful to not become impatient and try to work things out our own way. We must wait patiently and trust God.

Pray

This week, place in the Lord's hands anything about which you are anxious. Ask Him to give you a heart of trust in the right timing of His actions on your behalf. Pray that you will wait in faith to see the fulfillment of His promises. Pray that your children will see the patience of God in delaying Christ's return and seriously consider their spiritual state.

---

93 Genesis 27

Faithful to All His Promises

Ask

What are some things that only last for a little while?

The Bible tells us about something that lasts forever.

> *The grass withers, the flower fades, but the word of our God will stand forever. (Isaiah 40:8)*

Discuss

- What is this verse teaching us when it tells us that the grass withers and the flower fades?

- What is the promise in this verse?

- Why is it good that God's Word stands forever? What would be different if God's Word was not sure, but changed?

- How do you know that you can trust God's Word? Do you have any doubts we can pray about?

Read

Can you imagine living in a world where nothing is impossible? That is God's world! Nothing is impossible for Him. This amazing truth is displayed throughout the Bible in the mighty acts of God.

One of these wonderful, mighty acts is when God gave a 100-year-old man and a 90-year-old woman a baby.[94] Why did He do this? To show His power and to keep His promise. God's promise to make of Abraham a great nation started with the miracle birth of a baby

---

94 Genesis 21:1-7

boy, and 700 years later Joshua reminded the offspring of Abraham that God had not failed in any of His promises to them![95] This is amazing. God is faithful to His all promises. His words stand forever. Let's rejoice together that:

> *The grass withers, the flower fades, but the word of our God will stand forever. (Isaiah 40:8)*

For Younger Children: What would it be like to live in a world where nothing is impossible? That would be an amazing world! That is the world that God lives in! Nothing is impossible for Him. All His mighty acts in the Bible show us that God can do anything.

One of God's mighty acts is when He gave 100-year-old Abraham and 90-year-old Sarah a baby! Why did God wait so long to keep this promise to give them a child? God wanted to show His power. He wanted to teach Abraham to trust Him—even if it meant waiting a long time.

God promised Abraham that He would make a great nation from his family. Seven hundred years after Isaac was born, Joshua reminded the nation of Israel (Abraham's family) that God had not forgotten or failed in any of His promises to them! That is amazing! God kept every single one of His promises to Israel. God has made other promises to His children and God will keep every one of them. His Word stands forever.

Pray

This week thank God for the eternality of His Word and His faithfulness to His promises. Pray that your children would grasp the reality of God's faithfulness to His Word.

---

95 Joshua 24:2-3

Trusting in the Promises

Ask

What are some things you hope for? Are you sure that any of them will happen?

The Bible talks about being sure of something.

> *Now faith is the assurance of things hoped for, the conviction of things not seen. (Hebrews 11:1)*

Discuss

- What does the writer of Hebrews say about faith? Explain.

- How can you be sure of things you hope for and things you have not seen?[96]

- What are some things that we believe by faith?

- How do we know if we have faith in God's Word?[97]

- Does true faith mean we never have any doubts? Explain your answer.

- What can you do about your doubts?

Read

Abraham had great challenges to his faith. Though God had given him the promise to make of him a great nation, God did not give

---

96 Make sure your children understand that you can be sure of things you hope for and have not seen if what you hope for and haven't seen is what the Bible promises and says is true. Faith is having confidence in God's Word—what God says is true. If time and your children's maturity permit, you may want to look at Hebrews 11 together.

97 Help your children to understand that true faith involves obedience to God's Word. Our obedience is an indication of our belief.

him an heir until he was 100 years old.[98] Then, when the evidence that the promise would be fulfilled could be easily seen, God asked Abraham to sacrifice Isaac, the heir to the promise. Once again, Abraham's faith was put to the test.[99]

Would he trust God? Would he step out in obedience without being able to see the end result? Hebrews shows us the great faith that Abraham had: "He considered that God was able even to raise him from the dead" (Hebrews 11:19a). Surely a faith like that must come from a lifetime of stepping out in faith and obedience, and seeing God to be faithful.

If we want the kind of faith that Abraham had, we too must be willing to step out in faith and obedience and see God work for us. Human nature tends to play it safe. We like to *have all our ducks in a row.* But the life of faith compels us to trust God without seeing the end result—to step out and see that He is who He says He is, and He is faithful to all His promises.

> *Now faith is the assurance of things hoped for, the conviction of things not seen. (Hebrews 11:1)*

For Younger Children: Do you think Abraham ever had doubts? Even though God had promised that a great nation would come from Abraham, God did not give Abraham a child until he was 100 years old. Then God asked Abraham to give up his son, Isaac. So Abraham's faith was tested. Would he truly believe that God would keep His promise?

The Bible tells us that Abraham believed that God could even raise Isaac from the dead to make a great nation for Abraham. This kind of faith comes from many experiences of trusting God, obeying Him, and seeing God be faithful.

Do you want that kind of faith? Faith is a gift that God gives. Ask God for the gift of faith and be ready to see that God is who He says He is.

---

98 Genesis 21:5
99 Genesis 22:1-18

Pray

Pray this week that God will increase your faith. Ask Him to give you an obedient heart that flows from trust in Him. Pray that your children will see God as trustworthy and desire to grow in faith in Him.

Failure to Trust in the Promises

Ask

What do you think of when you hear the word "sin"?

Here is something the Bible tells us about sin:

> *For whatever does not proceed from faith is sin. (Romans 14:23b)*

Discuss

- What does this verse tell us about sin? What does this mean?[100]

- Why would not trusting God's promises be sinful?[101]

- Can you think of anyone in the Bible who did not believe God's promise or His Word? What was the consequence?[102]

- What is an example of when you trusted God's Word?[103] What helped you to trust God?

- Is there anything you are having a hard time trusting God for? Explain.

Read

God is completely trustworthy, and His promises are sure, and yet we sometimes doubt His promises. The way we act in response to

---

100 Though in Romans 14:23 Paul is addressing a specific situation of not causing a brother to stumble by what we eat or drink or don't eat or drink, nevertheless, Paul is making a universal point that "whatever does not proceed from faith is sin." In other words, any actions we take that do not come from a heart of faith and love for God are sinful.

101 Make sure your child understands that not trusting God's promises is unbelief; it is considering God untrustworthy.

102 Some possible examples: 10 spies; Adam and Eve; Lot's wife; Zechariah; Aaron and Miriam (when they did not trust God's choice of Moses as a leader)

103 Be ready to share an example from your own life.

His promises shows whether we truly believe God's promises. We can respond with faith that results in positive action, or we can respond in unbelief that results in consequences.

These two responses are demonstrated in the lives of Noah and Zechariah. Noah heard the word of the Lord and started building an ark—putting his faith into action.[104] Zechariah received the angel's message about God's promised son to him and Elizabeth, and he questioned it.[105] The result of his unbelief is that he was mute until John the Baptist was born. How do you most often respond to the promises God has made in His Word? Are you like Noah or like Zechariah?

May the Lord bless us with Noah-like faith that overflows in acting upon His Word that, in turn, overflows in encouraging others to trust God. May they see in us a heart of faith and actions of obedience that please our God.

For Younger Children: God can always be trusted. His promises are true. But sometimes we doubt God's promises. How do we know if we really believe God's promises? We can tell if we truly trust God's promises by the way we act.

Noah listened to God's word and started to build an ark. His faith in God's word caused him to act in obedience. Zechariah was given God's message by an angel who told him that he would have a son. But Zechariah did not believe the message. Because he did not believe God, he could not talk until John the Baptist was born.

We should ask, "Am I more like Noah or like Zechariah?" God knows our weakness and that sometimes it is hard for us to trust Him. Do you want to have a deeper trust in God? Ask God for the faith to trust Him. He loves to answer that prayer!

---

104 Genesis 6:9-22
105 Luke 1:5-25

Pray

Pray that God will increase your faith and that you would be a good testimony of trusting in God and acting upon His Word. Pray that your children will trust God and act on His Word.

Fighting the Fight of Faith

Ask

What is armor?[106]

If you are a Christian, you have armor, too. But it is a different kind of armor.

> *Finally, be strong in the Lord and in the strength of his might.*
> *[11]Put on the whole armor of God, that you may be able to stand*
> *against the schemes of the devil. (Ephesians 6:10-11)*

Discuss

- What kind of armor is Paul talking about in Ephesians?

- Why do we need armor?

- How does Satan fight against us?

- Do you live like you understand that you are always in a spiritual battle? What would help you to remember and recognize the battle you are in?

Read

Listening to our feelings and entertaining the doubts that Satan throws in his fiery darts causes a lot of problems for the Christian. But God has given us spiritual weapons to fight spiritual battles. Our faith is not a feeling—it is founded on real, solid truth. God's truth defeats the enemy of our souls. The Word of God is a powerful weapon against the lies of Satan and our lying emotions. The Holy

---

106 Armor is a covering for the body made of metal, wood, or leather used as protection against enemy weapons.

Spirit fights for us, and God Himself will be our strength if we confess our need of Him. We do not fight our battles alone!

God has also given us other Christians to strengthen us in battle—reminding us of the promises of God, strengthening us with the Word, holding us up in prayer. But we must not be passive in this battle, battered about by doubt, fear, and worry. We must be aggressive; soldiers don't sit passively on the sidelines. Like Asaph,[107] we must recall the mighty deeds of the Lord—both from the Bible and in our own lives. God is a mighty God who does not lose battles. Run to Him as you face the battles in your life.

For Younger Children: When we trust our feelings instead of what we know is true, we get in trouble. Satan loves to make us doubt God. But God has given His children spiritual weapons to fight the fight of faith. Faith is not a feeling. It is believing what is really true. We can use what we know is true from the Bible to fight the lies of Satan. God will help us fight for faith if we ask Him to help us. We do not need to fight alone!

We can also ask others to pray for us. We can also ask them to remind us of promises and other verses in the Bible. Remembering the mighty acts of God can help us to trust Him, too. God is a mighty God who does not lose any battles. He can help you with the battles in your life. Ask Him for His help today.

Pray

Pray that God will strengthen you for the battles you face. Ask Him to make you aggressive in the fight of faith and disciplined in it. Pray that your children will understand that there is a battle for their souls and only God can win that battle for them.

---

107 Psalm 75:1

DAY 38

Standing on the Promises of God

Ask

Do you know what the expression the last man standing means?[108]

God's Word shows us how to be a winner in the fight of faith.

> *Every word of God proves true; he is a shield to those who take refuge in him. (Proverbs 30:5)*

Discuss

- How can this verse help you fight the fight of faith?[109]

- What action does this verse show us is needed on our part?[110]

- What do you know about God's Word that tells you that you can trust it?[111]

- What are some promises you can stand on? (What are some promises you can memorize and remember to help you stand firm in faith?)

---

108 It means that the person is the winner in a fight or competition, that person is the last one left, that everyone else has dropped out or been defeated.

109 Make sure your children understand that we win spiritual battles when we stand firmly on the truth of the Word of God—when we trust that God's Word is completely true. We also win spiritual battles when we ask God for help and trust Him to be faithful in helping us. Reminding ourselves of this verse can strengthen us.

110 Your children should understand that it is not enough just to know this verse. Your children must take the initiative to ask God for help—they must take refuge in God. They should also find verses that will help them to know what is true and give them a weapon against the enemy's lies.

111 Make sure your children understand that God's Word does not change; it is backed up by the truthfulness, power, wisdom, and faithfulness of God; that it has been tested and proven true—we have a whole Bible full of history to show us this.

Read

Do you ever put yourself in the place of the 12 spies?[112] We can criticize Israel for not obeying God, and yet we are sometimes overcome with fear, choosing to look at the giants in our lives rather than stand on the promises of God. We really don't know if we would have stood with the confidence of Joshua and Caleb or cowered in fear and unbelief like the other spies.

What we do know from our vantage point is that the unbelief of Israel resulted in the consequence of wandering in the desert for 40 years, and that no spy who brought back a bad report entered the Promised Land.[113] This should sober us. How much blessing from God do we miss out on because we do not stand in confidence on His Word? God's Word is unchanging, unshakable, and completely reliable, because it is a reflection of His very nature. Oh, that we would in great confidence base our actions on the firm conviction that:

> *Every word of God proves true; he is a shield to those who take refuge in him. (Proverbs 30:5)*

For Younger Children: When you think about the story of the 12 spies going to check out Canaan, do you ever wonder if you would have been like Joshua and Caleb or like the 10 spies who were afraid to trust God? We would like to think that we would be like Joshua and Caleb, but we know that we are sometimes afraid. Sometimes the things we fear look so big to us that we fail to stand firmly on the promises of God. So we don't really know which side we would have been on.

We do know that because the people of Israel did not trust God's promise to give them the Promised Land, they had to wander in the desert for 40 years. All 10 of the men who did not trust God's promise were not allowed to enter the Promised Land. They all died while they were in the wilderness. That is so sad. Think about what they missed because they did not trust God. We don't want to be like them—missing what God has promised because we do not believe Him.

---

112 Numbers 13
113 Numbers 14:21-23

Remember that God's Word does not change. It is completely true, and we can trust it because God is truthful and unchanging. Trust in God's promises, and be among the last men standing! Fight the fight of faith and be a winner by making God your refuge.

Pray

This week, pray that God would give you the courage to stand on His Word. Pray that your children will be convinced that the Bible is true, and that they can put their full confidence in God.

Trusting in the Promises Leads to Obedience

Ask

What have you learned about faith from this book?

Here is an important Bible verse about faith:

> *So faith comes from hearing, and hearing through the word of Christ. (Romans 10:17)*

Discuss

- What does this verse tell you about faith? What does this verse mean when it says "hearing"?[114]

- Many people *hear* God's Word but don't believe it or trust Him. How can you tell if you hear and believe, or just hear?[115]

- Do you want to ask God for the gift of faith?

Read

"But at your word I will let down the nets" (Luke 5:5b). This is more than a simple acquiescence to a desire that Jesus expressed. It is an expression of understanding that Jesus is the Master (Luke 5:5a), and a confidence in His word. It is an expression of obedience that comes

---

114 Make sure that your children understand that this verse is not only talking about hearing with your ears (which is needed) but, as the rest of the chapter shows, it also implies that you are accepting what is being said. You agree with it and are committed to the truth.

115 A sign that we trust God's Word is that we obey it. Make sure your children understand that the people of Israel heard God's Word, but many hardened their hearts. They had "eyes that would not see and ears that would not hear" (Romans 11:8). We cannot make ourselves believe God's Word, but we can pray that God will give us open hearts to receive and trust His Word.

from trust. And it is an example to us of how we should respond to the commands of God. "At your word I will..."

Obedience is the natural outflow of faith. We see it in the life of Jesus, who went to the cross because He trusted His Father and obeyed His will. We don't see it in the people of Israel, who forgot their Savior, murmured in their tents, built an idol, and did not obey the Lord. Every day we have the choice of acting in unbelief, murmuring, and disobeying or acting in belief, "At your word I will..."

May Luke 5:5b be the refrain on our lips and in our hearts, the result of God's gracious gift of faith.

> *So faith comes from hearing, and hearing through the word of Christ. (Romans 10:17)*

For Younger Children: Jesus was standing in a boat when He taught a crowd of people. After He was done, He told Simon (Peter) to go to the deep part of the lake and put the nets into the water. Simon and the other fishermen had been fishing all night and hadn't caught any fish. They were tired and had already washed their nets. But Simon answered Jesus, "But at your word I will let down the nets." Simon understood that Jesus is the Master; He is in charge. Simon trusted Jesus' word when he obediently let down the nets. Do you know what happened then? The fishermen caught so many fish that their nets began to break!

We should obey Jesus like Simon did. Faith is hearing the Word of God, believing what it says, and obeying it. Every day you can choose either to obey or disobey what God tells us in the Bible. Like Simon, we should trust Jesus as our Master who knows what is best for us and is always right.

Pray

Pray that God would increase your faith this week and that you would have a heart of trust that leads to obedience. Ask God to give your children faith and the desire to read His Word.

Promise: Eternal Life

Ask

What do you know about heaven? What can you imagine heaven will be like?

Before Jesus died and returned to heaven, He told the disciples something about heaven.

> *"In my Father's house are many rooms. If it were not so, would I have told you that I go to prepare a place for you? ³And if I go and prepare a place for you, I will come again and will take you to myself, that where I am you may be also." (John 14:2-3)*

Discuss

- What is Jesus telling the disciples when He used the words "many rooms"?[116]

- What did Jesus mean when He said He was going to "prepare a place" for them? How was He going to do this?[117]

- What is the importance of this verse for us?[118]

- If you are a child of God, your real home is with Jesus in heaven. In what ways are Christians not at home in this world? What are you looking forward to in heaven?

---

116 Make sure that your children understand that Jesus is saying that there is plenty of room—there is a place for everyone who believes in Him.

117 Jesus was not building a physical place for them. He was preparing a way for them to live in heaven by dying on the cross for their sins. After Jesus died, the temple curtain was torn in two from top to bottom (Mark 15:38). This was to show that the way to God is now open to all who come to Him in faith.

118 Make sure your children understand that life on earth is for a short time and this world is full of brokenness. But life in heaven never ends, and it is wonderfully perfect as we enjoy our glorious God. There will be no tears, sorrow, sickness, or sin, just perfect fellowship with God and each other.

Read

For Christians, this world is not our home. We are strangers here "waiting for new heavens and a new earth in which righteousness dwells" according to God's promise (2 Peter 3:13). There is a reason we do not fit in, in this world—it is not home to us. We will be at home where righteousness reigns, the brokenness of this world has disappeared, and our King will reign.

Jesus is preparing a place for us in heaven, and someday He and will come back to bring us home. When He does, the Father will welcome each one of us with great joy for He is not ashamed to be called our God. What a great day that will be!

As we look forward to heaven, let us remember that trusting in the promises leads to obedience, which leads to great reward. That great reward is eternal life in heaven, the inheritance of every Christian.

For Younger Children: If you are a Christian, this world is not your real home. You are waiting to go to be with Jesus in heaven. In heaven, there will be no sin, evil, or death. All the sadness and brokenness of this world will be gone, and our King will rule forever.

Jesus made a way for us to be in heaven by dying on the cross to pay for our sins. If we trust in God's promises, we will obey Him and receive the great reward of living forever in heaven. Someday Jesus will return to bring everyone who trusts in Him to His home. God the Father, will welcome His children with great joy. What a great day that will be!

Pray

Pray that you will live with the constant understanding that heaven is the Christian's real home. Thank God for His promise of eternal life. Pray that your children will inherit the promise of eternal life and that God will be their God.

And this is the promise that he made to us— eternal life.

—1 John 2:25

Truth:78

ᴜr vision is that the next generations may know, honor, and treasure God, setting their hope in Christ alone, so that they will live as faithful disciples for the glory of God.

It is our mission to inspire and equip the church and home for the comprehensive discipleship of the next generation. To that end, we develop resources that put God at the center, focus on the gospel, and exalt Christ. They are grounded in sound doctrine for faithful discipleship.

Resources and Training Materials

Curriculum

We publish materials for formal Bible instruction in the classroom including Sunday School, Midweek Bible programs, Backyard Bible Clubs/VBS, and multi-age studies. The scope and sequence reflect our commitment to teach children and youth the whole counsel of God over the course of their education. Most materials can easily be adapted for use in Christian schools and homeschools.

Vision-Casting and Training

We offer a wide variety of booklets, video and audio seminars, articles, and other practical training resources designed to assist ministry leaders, volunteers, and parents to implement Truth78's vision and mission in their churches and homes. Many are available for free at Truth78.org.

Parenting and Family Discipleship

Truth78 equips parents to disciple their children with booklets, video presentations, family devotionals, children's books, articles, apps, and more. Curricula include take-home pages to help parents nurture faith at home by applying classroom lessons to their child's daily experience.

Bible Memory

Truth78 publishes Fighter Verses, the collection of 260 passages uniquely suited to arm individuals, families, and whole churches for the fight of faith. Companion resources include study guides, journals, coloring books, and songs to encourage Scripture memory, as well as Foundation Verses to help toddlers and preschoolers lay a firm biblical foundation.

For more information about resources and services, please contact us:

Truth78.org • info@Truth78.org
(877) 400-1414

GROWING IN THE WORD SER

God has given us in the Bible a book like no other, and we have been given the great responsibility and privilege to pass its life-giving truth to the next generation. The Growing in the Word Series aims to inspire and equip the church and home to teach the next generation to read and study the Bible, pray for understanding and a right heart, and apply what they learn to their daily lives.

Resources in this series provide an introduction to the Bible, its message, and use; a reading plan; help with Bible memory and Scripture-focused prayer; age-appropriate training toward biblical literacy; and inductive Bible study tools to help children and youth learn to read, observe, interpret, and apply the Bible to their everyday lives.

Help the children and youth in your home and church come to know and love God's Word and, more importantly, the God who reveals Himself through His Word. Their very life and eternal joy depend upon it!

The following booklets are included in the Growing in the Word Series:

- **From Childhood You Have Known:**
  Guiding Children to Understand and Treasure the Bible
- **The Inductive Bible Study Handbook:**
  Learn to Read, Observe, Interpret, and Apply the Bible
- **Meeting God in His Word:**
  A Guide to Bible Reading and Prayer for Children

Family Discipleship Collection

Inspiration and practical help for teaching and discipling children

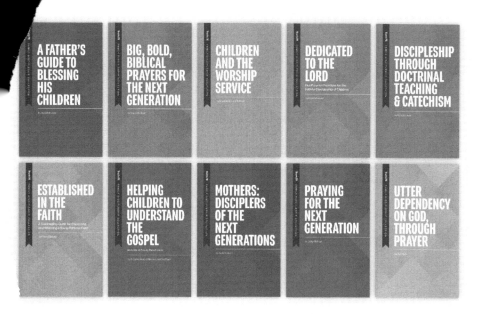

- A Father's Guide to Blessing His Children

- Big, Bold, Biblical Prayers for the Next Generation

- Children and the Worship Service

- Dedicated to the Lord: Five Parental Promises for the Faithful Discipleship of Children

- Discipleship through Doctrinal Teaching & Catechism

- Established in the Faith: A Discipleship Guide for Discerning and Affirming a Young Person's Faith

- Helping Children to Understand the Gospel

- Mothers: Disciplers of the Next Generations

- Praying for the Next Generation

- Utter Dependency on God, Through Prayer

Truth78.org/family-discipleship-collection

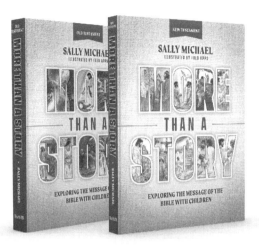

More Than a Story

Introduce children to a glorious God.

More Than a Story takes children (ages 6-12) on a chronological journey through the Bible with a God-centered, gospel-focused, discipleship-oriented, theologically grounded perspective.

Old Testament and New Testament volumes are available individually or as a bundle.

Truth78.org/more-than-a-story

Making HIM Known books

A series of books to teach children about the character and worth of God.

These illustrated family devotionals provide a way for the entire family to learn about our great God and His Word. Each chapter of these read-to and read-along books for elementary-age children ends with personal application and activities and is enhanced by full-color illustrations.

Each book is adapted from a Truth78 curriculum.

Truth78.org/making-him-known-series

Made in the USA
Columbia, SC
28 February 2023

13115534R00070